on
tremendous trifles

G.K. Chesterton
on
tremendous trifles

ET REMOTISSIMA PROPE

'on'

'on'

Published by Hesperus Press Limited
4 Rickett Street, London sw6 1ru
www.hesperuspress.com

First published in the *Daily News*, 1902–1909
This collection first published by Hesperus Press Limited, 2009

Foreword © Ben Schott, 2009

Designed and typeset by Fraser Muggeridge studio
Printed in Jordan by Jordan National Press

ISBN: 978-1-84391-606-2

Contents

Foreword

The essays herein were written between 1902 and 1909 for the *Daily News* – a Liberal paper founded by Charles Dickens in 1846 and bought in 1901 by the Quaker chocolatier George Cadbury. By the time the paper hired him as a columnist, G.K. Chesterton was a well-known writer and journalist. But under the *Daily News* masthead, and with the personal support of the new editor A.G. Gardiner, Chesterton's fame soared to new heights.

Soon, the iconic image of 'G.K.C.' – six foot four, twenty stone, sporting a wide-brimmed hat, pince-nez and capacious cloak, bowling down Fleet Street with his pockets jammed with papers – became the stuff of journalistic legend. Chesterton was, to some, no less than a Samuel Johnson for the Edwardian era. In at least eighty books, hundreds of poems, and 'a million' essays, Chesterton championed the axiom that the pen is mightier than the sword. Though, just in case this ever proved untrue, he habitually carried both a pocket knife and a swordstick.

Gilbert Keith Chesterton was born on 29th May 1874 in Kensington, London, the son of a prosperous estate agent. In his autobiography, Chesterton described his childhood as content and comfortable, and his youthful passion for fairy tales and toy theatres is reflected in a number of these essays. An ardent bookworm and vigorous debater, Chesterton was happy at St Paul's School, London, if not especially high-flying. At eighteen, he enrolled to study English, French and Latin at University College London, and art at the Slade. (Although he never pursued art as a profession, Chesterton continued to draw throughout his life and illustrated a number of publications, including novels by Hilaire Belloc and Edmund Bentley's collection of 'Clerihews'.)

From the time he left college in 1895 until his death some forty years later, Chesterton macerated himself in ink. From a lowly position as a publisher's reader he climbed the literary ladder with a speed and grace that defied his ever-increasing physical bulk. A swathe of essays and reviews was cemented in 1903 by a study of Robert Browning, and in 1904 by his first novel, *The Napoleon of Notting Hill*. Soon, nothing could halt his pen and the words came fast and sure (if not always fact-checked) in every conceivable form. Among his most popular and enduring works are a study of Charles Dickens (1906), *The Man Who Was Thursday* (1908), the Father Brown stories (from 1910), and books on St Francis of Assisi (1922), Chaucer (1932), and St Thomas Aquinas (1933).

Established as a writer, Chesterton quickly became a character – described by D.J. Conlon as 'forever stopping for a pork pie and a beer while he scribbled yet another poem or article on his cuff or on the back of a sugar packet.' Anthony Burgess noted that 'Chesterton belonged to an age when literary men could be public figures', and G.K.C. loomed large on the literary landscape alongside George Bernard Shaw, Hilaire Belloc and H.G. Wells.

Chesterton died at his home in Beaconsfield, Buckinghamshire, on 14th June 1936. In its obituary, *The Times* called him 'one of the chief figures in contemporary literature' and 'among the first essayists of his age.'

Chesterton was not afraid of the sub-clause and, to the modern eye, some of these essays tend towards the prolix. In one especially verbose sentence there are 13 commas, a pair of brackets, and a semicolon – within 108 words. Few editors working today would tolerate such orotundity, but then neither would they be thrilled by Chesterton's modus operandi. In a biography of Chesterton, A.S. Dale reported, 'The entire *Daily News* staff worried every Friday afternoon until his weekly copy finally arrived, and it never came the same way twice in a row.

Chesterton would scribble it on any kind paper – including wallpaper – and he would "walk it" there, or send it by messenger or cab, which might arrive with or without him. If Chesterton took a cab, he frequently had no money, so the staff had to pay the driver.'

A host of anecdotes testify that Chesterton's scatter-brained haphazardness was not confined to his work. On one famous occasion he sent his wife a telegram that read: 'Am at Market Harborough. Where ought I to be?' Her reply was 'Home.'

But if Chesterton's manner was chaotic, his mind was clear – a 'topsy-turvy' state of affairs which was mirrored in his work, where plucked memories and unlikely paradoxes are skilfully twisted to a sharp point. Chesterton once wrote that the best advice he could offer an aspiring journalist was to write an article for the *Sporting Times* and an article for the *Church Times* and then put them into the wrong envelopes. At his best, he achieved this trick within the space of a single essay.

Unlike many of his contemporaries, Chesterton was not a snob. He did not loathe the newly literate masses or their penny dreadfuls, nor did he have contempt for the suburb or the day-tripper. In fact, Chesterton took positive delight in the domestic and the day-to-day – so much so that, were it not for their erudition and wit, some of these essays might almost be Pooterish. (George and Weedon Grossmith's *The Diary of a Nobody* was published in 1892.)

Chesterton wrote of trains and taxis, shopping and pottering, trips to the country, games of croquet, the contents of his pockets, and lying in bed. His scale was human; his intent humane; his ideology rational, optimistic, moral, and democratic.

In *The Toy Theatre*, Chesterton asked, 'Has not everyone noticed how sweet and startling any landscape looks when seen though an arch?' And in each of these essays, Chesterton demonstrated a knack for reframing quotidian experience – just as Sherlock Holmes plucked the individual from the urban mass or, later, Jane Marple would extrapolate all of human nature from the sleepy village of St Mary Mead. 'To appreciate anything,' Chesterton wrote, 'we must always isolate it.'

Yet while Chesterton's subject matter was often the humdrum, the conclusions he drew were seldom dull. And, when they were, the verdict of A.N. Wilson is instructive: 'Chesterton being dull is livelier that most men's best.' (Chesterton himself said, 'They talk about things being as dull as ditchwater. For my part, I always think of ditchwater as teeming with quiet fun.') Chesterton's editor at the *Daily News* was only partly exaggerating when he said of his columnist, 'You may tap any subject you like, he will find a theme on which to hang all the mystery of time and eternity.'

In 1909, Chesterton published a selection of his *Daily News* articles under the characteristically oxymoronic title *Tremendous Trifles*. The critical reaction was mixed. The *New York Times* argued 'Mr Chesterton's clever juggling is not an exhibition of verbal gymnastics or a pastime merely, but a weapon of truth and sanity.' Yet in a pretty devastating review, *The Times Literary Supplement* said that while some of the individual essays 'are often as provocative as they are charming,' their parts 'might be transposed almost indefinitely without detection.' That there is some truth in this charge means we need not be unduly concerned that this volume contains twenty-one essays from the original selection of thirty-nine.

In a short preface to *Tremendous Trifles*, Chesterton wrote: 'These fleeting sketches... amount to no more than a sort of sporadic diary – a diary recording one day in twenty which happened to stick in the fancy – the only kind of diary the author has ever been able to keep. Even that diary he could only keep by keeping it in public, for bread and cheese.' This coy allusion to financial reward reminds us that these essays were work for hire, written against the deadlines and constraints of a column that had to be fed with 1,200–1,500 words every week. The *TLS* reviewer said 'he writes in impulsive gushes without apparently valuing any one idea above another.'

So, if some of these essays seem dashed-off in parts, they probably were.

There are kernels of profundity within *On Tremendous Trifles* – alongside elegantly turned logic and phrases. Yet the collection might best be appreciated now as a period piece – one that casts light on the texture of Edwardian Britain, the character of pre-First World War jobbing journalism, and the early and sincere thinking of one of Britain's great men of letters.

– Ben Schott, 2009

On Tremendous Trifles

Tremendous Trifles

Once upon a time there were two little boys who lived chiefly in the front garden, because their villa was a model one. The front garden was about the same size as the dinner table; it consisted of four strips of gravel, a square of turf with some mysterious pieces of cork standing up in the middle and one flower bed with a row of red daisies. One morning while they were at play in these romantic grounds, a passing individual, probably the milkman, leaned over the railing and engaged them in philosophical conversation. The boys, whom we will call Paul and Peter, were at least sharply interested in his remarks. For the milkman (who was, I need hardly say, a fairy) did his duty in that state of life by offering them in the regulation manner anything that they chose to ask for. And Paul closed with the offer with a businesslike abruptness, explaining that he had long wished to be a giant that he might stride across continents and oceans and visit Niagara or the Himalayas in an afternoon dinner stroll. The milkman producing a wand from his breast pocket, waved it in a hurried and perfunctory manner; and in an instant the model villa with its front garden was like a tiny doll's house at Paul's colossal feet. He went striding away with his head above the clouds to visit Niagara and the Himalayas. But when he came to the Himalayas, he found they were quite small and silly-looking, like the little cork rockery in the garden; and when he found Niagara it was no bigger than the tap turned on in the bathroom. He wandered round the world for several minutes trying to find something really large and finding everything small, till in sheer boredom he lay down on four or five prairies and fell asleep. Unfortunately his head was just outside the hut of an intellectual backwoodsman who came out of it at that moment with an axe in one hand and a book of Neo-Catholic Philosophy in the other. The man looked at the book and then at the giant, and then at the book again. And in the book it said, 'It can be maintained that the evil of pride consists in being out of proportion to the universe.' So the backwoodsman put down his book, took his axe and, working eight hours a day for about a week, cut the giant's head off; and there was an end of him.

Such is the severe yet salutary history of Paul. But Peter, oddly enough, made exactly the opposite request; he said he had long wished to be a pigmy about half an inch high; and of course he immediately became one. When the transformation was over he found himself in the midst of an immense plain, covered with a tall green jungle above which, at intervals, rose strange trees each with a head like the sun in symbolic pictures, with gigantic rays of silver and a huge heart of gold. Toward the middle of this prairie stood up a mountain of such romantic and impossible shape, yet of such stony height and dominance, that it looked like some incident of the end of the world. And far away on the faint horizon he could see the line of another forest, taller and yet more mystical, of a terrible crimson colour, like a forest on fire for ever. He set out on his adventures across that coloured plain; and he has not come to the end of it yet.

Such is the story of Peter and Paul, which contains all the highest qualities of a modern fairy tale, including that of being wholly unfit for children; and indeed the motive with which I have introduced it is not childish, but rather full of subtlety and reaction. It is in fact the almost desperate motive of excusing or palliating the pages that follow. Peter and Paul are the two primary influences upon European literature today; and I may be permitted to put my own preference in its most favourable shape, even if I can only do it by what little girls call telling a story.

I need scarcely say that I am the pigmy. The only excuse for the scraps that follow is that they show what can be achieved with a commonplace existence and the sacred spectacles of exaggeration. The other great literary theory, that which is roughly represented in England by Mr Rudyard Kipling, is that we moderns are to regain the primal zest by sprawling all over the world growing used to travel and geographical variety, being at home everywhere, that is being at home nowhere. Let it be granted that a man in a frock coat is a heartrending sight; and the two alternative methods still remain. Mr Kipling's school advises us to go to Central Africa in order to find a man without a frock coat. The school to which I belong suggests that we should stare steadily at the man until we see the man inside the frock coat. If we stare at him long enough he may even be moved to take off his coat to us; and that is a far greater compliment than his taking off his hat. In other words, we may, by fixing our attention almost fiercely on the facts actually before us, force them to turn into adventures; force them to give up their meaning and fulfil their mysterious purpose. The purpose of the Kipling literature is to show how many extraordinary things a man may see if he is active and strides from continent to continent like the giant in my tale. But the object of my school is to show how many extra-ordinary things even a lazy and ordinary man may see if he can spur himself to the single activity of seeing. For this purpose I have taken the laziest person of my acquaintance, that is myself; and made an idle diary of such odd things as I have fallen over by accident, in walking in a very limited area at a very indolent pace. If anyone says that these are very small affairs talked about in very big language, I can only gracefully compliment him upon seeing the joke. If anyone says that I am making mountains out of molehills, I confess with pride that it is so. I can imagine no more successful and productive form of manufacture than that of making mountains out of molehills. But I would add this not unimportant fact, that molehills are mountains; one has only to become a pigmy like Peter to discover that.

I have my doubts about all this real value in mountaineering, in getting to the top of everything and overlooking everything. Satan was the most celebrated of Alpine guides, when he took Jesus to the top of an exceeding high mountain and showed him all the kingdoms of the earth. But the joy of Satan in standing on a peak is not a joy in largeness, but a joy in beholding smallness, in the fact that all men look like insects at his feet. It is from the valley that things look large; it is from the level that things look high; I am a child of the level and have no need of that celebrated Alpine guide. I will lift up my eyes to the hills, from whence cometh my help; but I will not lift up my carcass to the hills, unless it is absolutely necessary. Everything is in an attitude of mind; and at this moment I am in a comfortable attitude. I will sit still and let the marvels and the adventures settle on me like flies. There are plenty of them, I assure you. The world will never starve for want of wonders, but only for want of wonder.

A Piece of Chalk

I remember one splendid morning, all blue and silver, in the summer holidays when I reluctantly tore myself away from the task of doing nothing in particular, and put on a hat of some sort and picked up a walking stick, and put six very bright-coloured chalks in my pocket. I then went into the kitchen (which, along with the rest of the house, belonged to a very square and sensible old woman in a Sussex village), and asked the owner and occupant of the kitchen if she had any brown paper. She had a great deal; in fact, she had too much; and she mistook the purpose and the rationale of the existence of brown paper.

She seemed to have an idea that if a person wanted brown paper he must be wanting to tie up parcels; which was the last thing I wanted to do; indeed, it is a thing which I have found to be beyond my mental capacity. Hence she dwelt very much on the varying qualities of toughness and endurance in the material. I explained to her that I only wanted to draw pictures on it, and that I did not want them to endure in the least; and that from my point of view, therefore, it was a question, not of tough consistency, but of responsive surface, a thing comparatively irrelevant in a parcel. When she understood that I wanted to draw she offered to overwhelm me with notepaper, apparently supposing that I did my notes and correspondence on old brown paper wrappers from motives of economy.

I then tried to explain the rather delicate logical shade, that I not only liked brown paper, but liked the quality of brownness in paper, just as I liked the quality of brownness in October woods, or in beer, or in the peat streams of the North. Brown paper represents the primal twilight of the first toil of creation, and with a bright-coloured chalk or two you can pick out points of fire in it, sparks of gold, and blood-red, and sea-green, like the first fierce stars that sprang out of divine darkness. All this I said (in an offhand way) to the old woman; and I put the brown paper in my pocket along with the chalks, and possibly other things. I suppose everyone must have reflected how primeval and how poetical are the things that one carries in one's pocket; the pocket knife, for instance, the type of all human tools, the infant of the sword. Once I planned to write a book of poems entirely about the things in my pockets. But I found it would be too long; and the age of the great epics is past.

With my stick and my knife, my chalks and my brown paper, I went out on to the great downs. I crawled across those colossal contours that express the best quality of England, because they are at the same time soft and strong. The smoothness of them has the same meaning as the smoothness of great carthorses, or the smoothness of the beech tree; it declares in the teeth of our timid and cruel theories that the mighty are merciful. As my eye swept the landscape, the landscape was as kindly as any of its cottages, but for power it was like an earthquake. The villages in the immense valley were safe, one could see, for centuries; yet the lifting of the whole land was like the lifting of one enormous wave to wash them all away.

I crossed one swell of living turf after another, looking for a place to sit down and draw. Do not, for heaven's sake, imagine I was going to sketch from nature. I was going to draw devils and seraphim, and blind old gods that men worshipped before the dawn of right, and saints in robes of angry crimson, and seas of strange green, and all the sacred or monstrous symbols that look so well in bright colours on brown paper. They are much better worth drawing than nature; also they are much easier to draw. When a cow came slouching by in the field next to me, a mere artist might have drawn it; but I always get wrong in the hind legs of quadrupeds. So I drew the soul of the cow; which I saw there plainly walking before me in the sunlight; and the soul was all purple and silver, and had seven horns and the mystery that belongs to all the beasts. But though I could not with a crayon get the best out of the landscape, it does not follow that the landscape was not getting the best out of me. And this,

8

I think, is the mistake that people make about the old poets who lived before Wordsworth, and were supposed not to care very much about nature because they did not describe it much.

They preferred writing about great men to writing about great hills; but they sat on the great hills to write it. They gave out much less about nature, but they drank in, perhaps, much more. They painted the white robes of their holy virgins with the blinding snow, at which they had stared all day. They blazoned the shields of their paladins with the purple and gold of many heraldic sunsets. The greenness of a thousand green leaves clustered into the live green figure of Robin Hood. The blueness of a score of forgotten skies became the blue robes of the Virgin. The inspiration went in like sunbeams and came out like Apollo.

But as I sat scrawling these silly figures on the brown paper, it began to dawn on me, to my great disgust, that I had left one chalk, and that a most exquisite and essential chalk, behind. I searched all my pockets, but I could not find any white chalk. Now, those who are acquainted with all the philosophy (nay, religion) which is typified in the art of drawing on brown paper, know that white is positive and essential. I cannot avoid remarking here upon a moral significance. One of the wise and awful truths which this brown paper art reveals, is this, that white is a colour. It is not a mere absence of colour; it is a shining and affirmative thing, as fierce as red, as definite as black. When, so to speak, your pencil grows red-hot, it draws roses; when it grows white-hot, it draws stars. And one of the two or three defiant verities of the best religious morality, of real Christianity, for example, is exactly this same thing; the chief assertion of religious morality is that white is a colour. Virtue is not the absence of vices or the avoidance of moral dangers; virtue is a vivid and separate thing, like pain or a particular smell. Mercy does not mean not being cruel or sparing people revenge or punishment; it means a plain and positive thing like the sun, which one has either seen or not seen.

9

Chastity does not mean abstention from sexual wrong; it means something flaming, like Joan of Arc. In a word, God paints in many colours; but He never paints so gorgeously, I had almost said so gaudily, as when He paints in white. In a sense our age has realised this fact, and expressed it in our sullen costume. For if it were really true that white was a blank and colourless thing, negative and non-committal, then white would be used instead of black and grey for the funeral dress of this pessimistic period. We should see city gentlemen in frock coats of spotless silver linen, with top hats as white as wonderful arum lilies. Which is not the case.

Meanwhile, I could not find my chalk.

I sat on the hill in a sort of despair. There was no town nearer than Chichester at which it was even remotely probable that there would be such a thing as an artist's colourman. And yet, without white, my absurd little pictures would be as pointless as the world would be if there were no good people in it. I stared stupidly round, racking my brain for expedients. Then I suddenly stood up and roared with laughter, again and again, so that the cows stared at me and called a committee. Imagine a man in the Sahara regretting that he had no sand for his hourglass. Imagine a gentleman in mid-ocean wishing that he had brought some salt water with him for his chemical experiments. I was sitting on an immense warehouse of white chalk. The landscape was made entirely out of white chalk. White chalk was piled more miles until it met the sky. I stooped and broke a piece off the rock I sat on; it did not mark so well as the shop chalks do; but it gave the effect. And I stood there in a trance of pleasure, realising that this Southern England is not only a grand peninsula, and a tradition and a civilisation; it is something even more admirable. It is a piece of chalk.

The Secret of a Train

All this talk of a railway mystery has sent my mind back to a loose memory. I will not merely say that this story is true: because, as you will soon see, it is all truth and no story. It has no explanation and no conclusion; it is, like most of the other things we encounter in life, a fragment of something else which would be intensely exciting if it were not too large to be seen. For the perplexity of life arises from there being too many interesting things in it for us to be interested properly in any of them; what we call its triviality is really the tag-ends of numberless tales; ordinary and unmeaning existence is like ten thousand thrilling detective stories mixed up with a spoon. My experience was a fragment of this nature, and it is, at any rate, not fictitious. Not only am I not making up the incidents (what there were of them), but I am not making up the atmosphere of the landscape, which were the whole horror of the thing. I remember them vividly, and they were as I shall now describe.

About noon of an ashen autumn day some years ago I was standing outside the station at Oxford intending to take the train to London. And for some reason, out of idleness or the emptiness of my mind or the emptiness of the pale grey sky, or the cold, a kind of caprice fell upon me that I would not go by that train at all, but would step out on the road and walk at least some part of the way to London. I do not know if other people are made like me in this matter; but to me it is always dreary weather, what may be called useless weather, that slings into life a sense of action and romance. On bright blue days I do not want anything to happen; the world is complete and beautiful, a thing for contemplation. I no more ask for adventures under that turquoise dome than I ask for adventures in church. But when the background of man's life is a grey background, then, in the name of man's sacred supremacy, I desire to paint on it in fire and gore. When the heavens fail man refuses to fail; when the sky seems to have written on it, in letters of lead and pale silver, the decree that nothing shall happen, then the immortal soul, the prince of the creatures, rises up and decrees that something shall happen, if it be only the slaughter of a policeman. But this is a digressive way of stating what I have said already – that the bleak sky awoke in me a hunger for some change of plans, that the monotonous weather seemed to render unbearable the use of the monotonous train, and that I set out into the country lanes, out of the town of Oxford. It was, perhaps, at that moment that a strange curse came upon me out of the city and the sky, whereby it was decreed that years afterwards I should, in an article in the *Daily News*, talk about Sir George Trevelyan in connection with Oxford, when I knew perfectly well that he went to Cambridge.

As I crossed the country everything was ghostly and colourless. The fields that should have been green were as grey as the skies; the treetops that should have been green were as grey as the clouds and as cloudy. And when I had walked for some hours the evening was closing in. A sickly sunset clung weakly to the horizon, as if pale with reluctance to leave the world in the dark. And as it faded more and more the skies seemed to come closer and to threaten. The clouds which had been merely sullen became swollen; and then they loosened and let down the dark curtains of the rain. The rain was blinding and seemed to beat like blows from an enemy at close quarters; the skies seemed bending over and bawling in my ears. I walked on many more miles before I met a man, and in that distance my mind had been made up; and when I met him I asked him if anywhere in the neighbourhood I could pick up the train for Paddington. He directed me to a small silent station (I cannot even remember the name of it) which stood well away from the road and looked as lonely as a hut on the Andes. I do not think I have ever seen such a type of time and sadness and scepticism and everything devilish as that station was: it looked as if it had always been raining there ever since the creation of the world. The water streamed from the soaking wood of it as if it were not water at all, but some loathsome liquid corruption of the wood itself; as if the solid station were eternally falling to pieces and pouring away in filth. It took me nearly ten minutes to find a man in the station. When I did he was a dull one, and when I asked him if there was a train to Paddington his answer was sleepy and vague. As far as I understood him, he said there would be a train in half an hour. I sat down and lit a cigar and waited, watching the last tail of the tattered sunset and listening to the everlasting rain. It may have been in half an hour or less, but a train came rather slowly into the station. It was an unnaturally dark train; I could not see a light anywhere in the long black body of it; and I could not see any guard running beside it. I was reduced to walking up to the engine and calling out to the stoker to ask if the train was going to London. 'Well – yes, sir,' he said, with an unaccountable kind of reluctance. 'It is going to London; but –' It was just starting, and I jumped into the first carriage; it was pitch dark. I sat there smoking and wondering, as we steamed through the continually darkening landscape, lined with desolate poplars, until we slowed down and stopped, irrationally, in the middle of a field. I heard a heavy noise as of some one clambering off the train, and a dark, ragged head suddenly put itself into my window. 'Excuse me, sir,' said the stoker, 'but I think, perhaps – well, perhaps you ought to know – there's a dead man in this train.'

Had I been a true artist, a person of exquisite susceptibilities and nothing else, I should have been bound, no doubt, to be finally overwhelmed with this sensational touch, and to have insisted on getting out and walking. As it was, I regret to say, I expressed myself politely, but firmly, to the effect that I didn't care particularly if the train took me to Paddington. But when the train had started with its unknown burden I did do one thing, and do it quite instinctively, without stopping to think, or to think more than a flash. I threw away my cigar. Something that is as old as man and has to do with all mourning and ceremonial told me to do it. There was something unnecessarily horrible, it seemed to me, in the idea of there being only two men in that train, and one of them dead and the other smoking a cigar. And as the red and gold of the butt end of it faded like a funeral torch trampled out at some symbolic moment of a procession, I realised how immortal ritual is. I realised (what is the origin and essence of all ritual) that in the presence of those sacred riddles about which we can say nothing it is more decent merely to do something. And I realised that ritual will always mean throwing away something; *destroying* our corn or wine upon the altar of our gods.

When the train panted at last into Paddington Station I sprang out of it with a suddenly released curiosity. There was a barrier and officials guarding the rear part of the train; no one was allowed to press towards it. They were guarding and hiding something; perhaps death in some too shocking form, perhaps something like the Merstham matter, so mixed up with human mystery and wickedness that the land has to give it a sort of sanctity; perhaps something worse than either. I went out gladly enough into the streets and saw the lamps shining on the laughing faces. Nor have I ever known from that day to this into what strange story I wandered or what frightful thing was my companion in the dark.

The Perfect Game

We have all met the man who says that some odd things have happened to him, but that he does not really believe that they were supernatural. My own position is the opposite of this. I believe in the supernatural as a matter of intellect and reason, not as a matter of personal experience. I do not see ghosts; I only see their inherent probability. But it is entirely a matter of the mere intelligence, not even of the motions; my nerves and body are altogether of this earth, very earthy. But upon people of this temperament one weird incident will often leave a peculiar impression. And the weirdest circumstance that ever occurred to me occurred a little while ago. It consisted in nothing less than my playing a game, and playing it quite well for some seventeen consecutive minutes. The ghost of my grandfather would have astonished me less.

On one of these blue and burning afternoons I found myself, to my inexpressible astonishment, playing a game called croquet. I had imagined that it belonged to the epoch of Leach and Anthony Trollope, and I had neglected to provide myself with those very long and luxuriant side whiskers which are really essential to such a scene. I played it with a man whom we will call Parkinson, and with whom I had a semi-philosophical argument which lasted through the entire contest. It is deeply implanted in my mind that I had the best of the argument; but it is certain and beyond dispute that I had the worst of the game.

'Oh, Parkinson, Parkinson!' I cried, patting him affectionately on the head with a mallet, 'how far you really are from the pure love of the sport – you who can play. It is only we who play badly who love the game itself. You love glory; you love applause; you love the earthquake voice of victory; you do not love croquet. You do not love croquet until you love being beaten at croquet. It is we the bunglers who adore the occupation in the abstract. It is we to whom it is art for art's sake. If we may see the face of

Croquet herself (if I may so express myself) we are content to see her face turned upon us in anger. Our play is called amateurish; and we wear proudly the name of amateur, for amateurs is but the French for Lovers. We accept all adventures from our Lady, the most disastrous or the most dreary. We wait outside her iron gates (I allude to the hoops), vainly essaying to enter. Our devoted balls, impetuous and full of chivalry, will not be confined within the pedantic boundaries of the mere croquet ground. Our balls seek honour in the ends of the earth; they turn up in the flowerbeds and the conservatory; they are to be found in the front garden and the next street. No, Parkinson! The good painter has skill. It is the bad painter who loves his art. The good musician loves being a musician, the bad musician loves music. With such a pure and hopeless passion do I worship croquet. I love the game itself. I love the parallelogram of grass marked out with chalk or tape, as if its limits were the frontiers of my sacred Fatherland, the four seas of Britain. I love the mere swing of the mallets, and the click of the balls is music. The four colours are to me sacramental and symbolic, like the red of martyrdom, or the white of Easter Day. You lose all this, my poor Parkinson. You have to solace yourself for the absence of this vision by the paltry consolation of being able to go through hoops and to hit the stick.'

And I waved my mallet in the air with a graceful gaiety.

'Don't be too sorry for me,' said Parkinson, with his simple sarcasm. 'I shall get over it in time. But it seems to me that the more a man likes a game the better he would want to play it. Granted that the pleasure in the thing itself comes first, does not the pleasure of success come naturally and inevitably afterwards? Or, take your own simile of the Knight and his Lady-love. I admit the gentleman does first and foremost want to be in the lady's presence. But I never yet heard of a gentleman who wanted to look an utter ass when he was there.'

'Perhaps not; though he generally looks it,' I replied. 'But the truth is that there is a fallacy in the simile, although it was my own. The happiness at which the lover is aiming is an infinite happiness, which can be extended without limit. The more he is loved, normally speaking, the jollier he will be. It is definitely true that the stronger the love of both lovers, the stronger will be the happiness. But it is not true that the stronger the play of both croquet players the stronger will be the game. It is logically possible – (follow me closely here, Parkinson!) – it is logically possible, to play croquet too well to enjoy it at all. If you could put this blue ball through that distant hoop as easily as you could pick it up with your hand, then you would not put it through that hoop any more than you pick it up with your hand; it would not be worth doing. If you could play unerringly you would not play at all. The moment the game is perfect the game disappears.'

'I do not think, however,' said Parkinson, 'that you are in any immediate danger of effecting that sort of destruction. I do not think your croquet will vanish through its own faultless excellence. You are safe for the present.'

I again caressed him with the mallet, knocked a ball about, wired myself, and resumed the thread of my discourse.

The long, warm evening had been gradually closing in, and by this time it was almost twilight. By the time I had delivered four more fundamental principles, and my companion had gone through five more hoops, the dusk was verging upon dark.

'We shall have to give this up,' said Parkinson, as he missed a ball almost for the first time, 'I can't see a thing.'

'Nor can I,' I answered, 'and it is a comfort to reflect that I could not hit anything if I saw it.'

With that I struck a ball smartly, and sent it away into the darkness towards where the shadowy figure of Parkinson moved in the hot haze. Parkinson immediately uttered a loud and dramatic cry. The situation, indeed, called for it. I had hit the right ball.

Stunned with astonishment, I crossed the gloomy ground, and hit my ball again. It went through a hoop. I could not see the hoop; but it was the right hoop. I shuddered from head to foot.

Words were wholly inadequate, so I slouched heavily after that impossible ball. Again I hit it away into the night, in what I supposed was the vague direction of the quite invisible stick. And in the dead silence I heard the stick rattle as the ball struck it heavily.

I threw down my mallet. 'I can't stand this,' I said. 'My ball has gone right three times. These things are not of this world.'

'Pick your mallet up,' said Parkinson, 'have another go.'

'I tell you I daren't. If I made another hoop like that I should see all the devils dancing there on the blessed grass.'

'Why devils?' asked Parkinson, 'they may be only fairies making fun of you. They are sending you the "Perfect Game", which is no game.'

I looked about me. The garden was full of a burning darkness, in which the faint glimmers had the look of fire. I stepped across the grass as if it burnt me, picked up the mallet, and hit the ball somewhere – somewhere where another ball might be. I heard the dull click of the balls touching, and ran into the house like one pursued.

The Extraordinary Cabman

From time to time I have introduced into this newspaper column the narration of incidents that have really occurred. I do not mean to insinuate that in this respect it stands alone among newspaper columns. I mean only that I have found that my meaning was better expressed by some practical parable out of daily life than by any other method; therefore I propose to narrate the incident of the extraordinary cabman, which occurred to me only three days ago, and which, slight as it apparently is, aroused in me a moment of genuine emotion bordering upon despair.

On the day that I met the strange cabman I had been lunching in a little restaurant in Soho in company with three or four of my best friends. My best friends are all either bottom-less sceptics or quite uncontrollable believers, so our discussion at luncheon turned upon the most ultimate and terrible ideas. And the whole argument worked out ultimately to this: that the question is whether a man can be certain of anything at all. I think he can be certain, for if (as I said to my friend, furiously brandishing an empty bottle) it is impossible intellectually to entertain certainty, what is this certainty which it is impossible to entertain? If I have never experienced such a thing as certainty I cannot even say that a thing is not certain. Similarly, if I have never experienced such a thing as green I cannot even say that my nose is not green. It may be as green as possible for all I know, if I have really no experience of greenness. So we shouted at each other and shook the room; because metaphysics is the only thoroughly emotional thing. And the difference between us was very deep, because it was a difference as to the object of the whole thing called broadmindedness or the opening of the intellect. For my friend said that he opened his intellect as the sun opens the fans of a palm tree, opening for opening's sake, opening infinitely for ever. But I said that

I opened my intellect as I opened my mouth, in order to shut it again on something solid. I was doing it at the moment. And as I truly pointed out, it would look uncommonly silly if I went on opening my mouth infinitely, for ever and ever.

Now when this argument was over, or at least when it was cut short (for it will never be over), I went away with one of my companions, who in the confusion and comparative insanity of a General Election had somehow become a Member of Parliament, and I drove with him in a cab from the corner of Leicester Square to the members' entrance of the House of Commons, where the police received me with a quite unusual tolerance. Whether they thought that he was my keeper or that I was his keeper is a discussion between us which still continues.

It is necessary in this narrative to preserve the utmost exactitude of detail. After leaving my friend at the House I took the cab on a few hundred yards to an office in Victoria Street which I had to visit. I then got out and offered him more than his fare. He looked at it, but not with the surly doubt and general disposition to try it on which is not unknown among normal cabmen. But this was no normal, perhaps, no human, cabman. He looked at it with a dull and infantile astonishment, clearly quite genuine. 'Do you know, sir,' he said, 'you've only given me 1s. 8d?' I remarked, with some surprise, that I did know it. 'Now you know, sir,' said he in a kindly, appealing, reasonable way, 'you know that ain't the fare from Euston.' 'Euston,' I repeated vaguely, for the phrase at that moment sounded to me like China or Arabia. 'What on earth has Euston got to do with it?' 'You hailed me just outside Euston Station,' began the man with astonishing precision, 'and then you said –' 'What in the name of Tartarus are you talking about?' I said with Christian forbearance; 'I took you at the south-west corner of Leicester Square.' 'Leicester Square,' he exclaimed, loosening a kind of cataract of scorn, 'why we ain't been near Leicester Square today. You hailed me outside Euston Station, and you said –' 'Are you mad, or am I?' I asked with scientific calm.

I looked at the man. No ordinary dishonest cabman would think of creating so solid and colossal and creative a lie. And this man was not a dishonest cabman. If ever a human face was heavy and simple and humble, and with great big blue eyes protruding like a frog's, if ever (in short) a human face was all that a human face should be, it was the face of that resentful and respectful cabman. I looked up and down the street; an unusually dark twilight seemed to be coming on. And for one second the old nightmare of the sceptic put its finger on my nerve. What was certainty? Was anybody certain of anything? Heavens! to think of the dull rut of the sceptics who go on asking whether we possess a future life. The exciting question for real scepticism is whether we possess a past life. What is a minute ago, rationalistically considered, except a tradition and a picture? The darkness grew deeper from the road. The cabman calmly gave me the most elaborate details of the gesture, the words, the complex but consistent course of action which I had adopted since that remarkable occasion when I had hailed him outside Euston Station. How did I know (my sceptical friends would say) that I had not hailed him outside Euston? I was firm about my assertion; he was quite equally firm about his. He was obviously quite as honest a man as I, and a member of a much more respectable profession. In that moment the universe and the stars swung just a hair's breadth from their balance, and the foundations of the earth were moved. But for the same reason that I believe in Democracy, for the same reason that I believe in free will, for the same reason that I believe in fixed character of virtue, the reason that could only be expressed by saying that I do not choose to be a lunatic, I continued to believe that this honest cabman was wrong, and I repeated to him that I had really taken him at the corner of Leicester Square. He began with the same evident and ponderous sincerity, 'You hailed me outside Euston Station, and you said –'

And at this moment there came over his features a kind of frightful transfiguration of living astonishment, as if he had been lit up like a lamp from the inside. 'Why, I beg your pardon, sir,' he said. 'I beg your pardon. I beg your pardon. You took me from Leicester Square. I remember now. I beg your pardon.' And with that this astonishing man let out his whip with a sharp crack at his horse and went trundling away. The whole of which interview, before the banner of St George I swear, is strictly true.

I looked at the strange cabman as he lessened in the distance and the mists. I do not know whether I was right in fancying that although his face had seemed so honest there was something unearthly and demoniac about him when seen from behind. Perhaps he had been sent to tempt me from my adherence to those sanities and certainties which I had defended earlier in the day. In any case it gave me pleasure to remember that my sense of reality, though it had rocked for an instant, had remained erect.

An Accident

Some time ago I wrote in these columns an article called 'The Extraordinary Cabman'. I am now in a position to contribute my experience of a still more extraordinary cab. The extraordinary thing about the cab was that it did not like me; it threw me out violently in the middle of the Strand. If my friends who read the *Daily News* are as romantic (and as rich) as I take them to be, I presume that this experience is not uncommon. I suppose that they are all being thrown out of cabs all over London. Still, as there are some people, virginal and remote from the world, who have not yet had this luxurious experience, I will give a short account of the psychology of myself when my hansom cab ran into the side of a motor omnibus, and I hope hurt it.

I do not need to dwell on the essential romance of the hansom cab – that one really noble modern thing which our age, when it is judged, will gravely put beside the Parthenon. It is really modern in that it is both secret and swift. My particular hansom cab was modern in these two respects; it was also very modern in the fact that it came to grief. But it is also English; it is not to be found abroad; it belongs to a beautiful, romantic country where nearly everybody is pretending to be richer than they are, and acting as if they were. It is comfortable, and yet it is reckless; and that combination is the very soul of England. But although I had always realised all these good qualities in a hansom cab, I had not experienced all the possibilities, or, as the moderns put it, all the aspects of that vehicle. My enunciation of the merits of a hansom cab had been always made when it was the right way up. Let me, therefore, explain how I felt when I fell out of a hansom cab for the first and, I am happy to believe, the last time. Polycrates threw one ring into the sea to propitiate the Fates. I have thrown one hansom cab into the sea (if you will excuse a rather violent metaphor) and the Fates are, I am quite sure, propitiated. Though I am told they do not like to be told so.

I was driving yesterday afternoon in a hansom cab down one of the sloping streets into the Strand, reading one of my own admirable articles with continual pleasure, and still more continual surprise, when the horse fell forward, scrambled a moment on the scraping stones, staggered to his feet again, and went forward. The horses in my cabs often do this, and I have learnt to enjoy my own articles at any angle of the vehicle. So I did not see anything at all odd about the way the horse went on again. But I saw it suddenly in the faces of all the people on the pavement. They were all turned towards me, and they were all struck with fear suddenly, as with a white flame out of the sky. And one man half ran out into the road with a movement of the elbow as if warding off a blow, and tried to stop the horse. Then I knew that the reins were lost, and the next moment the horse was like a living thunderbolt. I try to describe things exactly as they seemed to me; many details I may have missed or misstated; many details may have, so to speak, gone mad in the race down the road. I remember that I once called one of my experiences narrated in this paper 'A Fragment of Fact'. This is, at any rate, a fragment of fact. No fact could possibly be more fragmentary than the sort of fact that I expected to be at the bottom of that street.

I believe in preaching to the converted; for I have generally found that the converted do not understand their own religion. Thus I have always urged in this paper that democracy has a deeper meaning than democrats understand; that is, that common and popular things, proverbs, and ordinary sayings always have something in them unrealised by most who repeat them. Here is one. We have all heard about the man who is in momentary danger, and who sees the whole of his life pass before him in a moment.

In the cold, literal, and common sense of words, this is obviously a thundering lie. Nobody can pretend that in an accident or a mortal crisis he elaborately remembered all the tickets he had ever taken to Wimbledon, or all the times that he had ever passed the brown bread and butter.

But in those few moments, while my cab was tearing towards the traffic of the Strand, I discovered that there is a truth behind this phrase, as there is behind all popular phrases. I did really have, in that short and shrieking period, a rapid succession of a number of fundamental points of view. I had, so to speak, about five religions in almost as many seconds. My first religion was pure Paganism, which among sincere men is more shortly described as extreme fear. Then there succeeded a state of mind which is quite real, but for which no proper name has ever been found. The ancients called it Stoicism, and I think it must be what some German lunatics mean (if they mean anything) when they talk about Pessimism. It was an empty and open acceptance of the thing that happens – as if one had got beyond the value of it. And then, curiously enough, came a very strong contrary feeling – that things mattered very much indeed, and yet that they were something more than tragic. It was a feeling, not that life was unimportant, but that life was much too important ever to be anything but life. I hope that this was Christianity. At any rate, it occurred at the moment when we went crash into the omnibus.

It seemed to me that the hansom cab simply turned over on top of me, like an enormous hood or hat. I then found myself crawling out from underneath it in attitudes so undignified that they must have added enormously to that great cause to which the Anti-Puritan League and I have recently dedicated ourselves. I mean the cause of the pleasures of the people. As to my demeanour when I emerged, I have two confessions to make, and they are both made merely in the interests of mental science. The first is that whereas I had been in a quite pious frame of mind the moment before the collision, when I got to my feet and found I had got off with a cut or two I began (like St Peter) to curse and to swear. A man offered me a newspaper or something that I had dropped. I can distinctly remember consigning the paper to a state of irremediable spiritual ruin. I am very sorry for this now, and I apologise both to the man and to the paper. I have not the least idea what was the meaning of this unnatural anger; I mention it as a psychological confession. It was immediately followed by extreme hilarity, and I made so many silly jokes to the policeman that he disgraced himself by continual laughter before all the little boys in the street, who had hitherto taken him seriously.

There is one other odd thing about the matter which I also mention as a curiosity of the human brain or deficiency of brain. At intervals of about every three minutes I kept on reminding the policeman that I had not paid the cabman, and that I hoped he would not lose his money. He said it would be all right, and the man would appear. But it was not until about half an hour afterwards that it suddenly struck me with a shock intolerable that the man might conceivably have lost more than half a crown; that he had been in danger as well as I. I had instinctively regarded the cabman as something uplifted above accidents, a god. I immediately made inquiries, and I am happy to say that they seemed to have been unnecessary.

But henceforward I shall always understand with a darker and more delicate charity those who take tythe of mint, and anise, and cumin, and neglect the weightier matters of the law; I shall remember how I was once really tortured with owing half a crown to a man who might have been dead. Some admirable men in white coats at the Charing Cross Hospital tied up my small injury, and I went out again into the Strand. I felt upon me even a kind of unnatural youth; I hungered for something untried. So to open a new chapter in my life I got into a hansom cab.

The Advantages of Having One Leg

A friend of mine who was visiting a poor woman in bereavement and casting about for some phrase of consolation that should not be either insolent or weak, said at last, 'I think one can live through these great sorrows and even be the better. What wears one is the little worries.' 'That's quite right, mum,' answered the old woman with emphasis, 'and I ought to know, seeing I've had ten of 'em.' It is, perhaps, in this sense that it is most true that little worries are most wearing. In its vaguer significance the phrase, though it contains a truth, contains also some possibilities of self-deception and error. People who have both small troubles and big ones have the right to say that they find the small ones the most bitter; and it is undoubtedly true that the back which is bowed under loads incredible can feel a faint addition to those loads; a giant holding up the earth and all its animal creation might still find the grasshopper a burden. But I am afraid that the maxim that the smallest worries are the worst is sometimes used or abused by people, because they have nothing but the very smallest worries. The lady may excuse herself for reviling the crumpled rose leaf by reflecting with what extraordinary dignity she would wear the crown of thorns – if she had to. The gentleman may permit himself to curse the dinner and tell himself that he would behave much better if it were a mere matter of starvation. We need not deny that the grasshopper on man's shoulder is a burden; but we need not pay much respect to the gentleman who is always calling out that he would rather have an elephant when he knows there are no elephants in the country. We may concede that a straw may break the camel's back, but we like to know that it really is the last straw and not the first.

I grant that those who have serious wrongs have a real right to grumble, so long as they grumble about something else. It is a singular fact that if they are sane they almost always do grumble about something else. To talk quite reasonably about your own quite real wrongs is the quickest way to go off your head. But people with great troubles talk about little ones, and the man who complains of the crumpled rose leaf very often has his flesh full of the thorns. But if a man has commonly a very clear and happy daily life then I think we are justified in asking that he shall not make mountains out of molehills. I do not deny that molehills can sometimes be important. Small annoyances have this evil about them, that they can be more abrupt because they are more invisible; they cast no shadow before, they have no atmosphere. No one ever had a mystical premonition that he was going to tumble over a hassock. William III died by falling over a molehill; I do not suppose that with all his varied abilities he could have managed to fall over a mountain. But when all this is allowed for, I repeat that we may ask a happy man (not William III) to put up with pure inconveniences, and even make them part of his happiness. Of positive pain or positive poverty I do not here speak. I speak of those innumerable accidental limitations that are always falling across our path – bad weather, confinement to this or that house or room, failure of appoint- ments or arrangements, waiting at railway stations, missing posts, finding unpunctuality when we want punctuality, or, what is worse, finding punctuality when we don't. It is of the poetic pleasures to be drawn from all these that I sing – I sing with confidence because I have recently been experimenting in the poetic pleasures which arise from having to sit in one chair with a sprained foot, with the only alternative course of standing on one leg like a stork – a stork is a poetic simile; therefore I eagerly adopted it.

To appreciate anything we must always isolate it, even if the thing itself symbolise something other than isolation. If we wish to see what a house is it must be a house in some uninhabited landscape. If we wish to depict what a man really is we must depict a man alone in a desert or on a dark sea sand. So long as he is a single figure he means all that humanity means; so long as he is solitary he means human society; so long as he is solitary he means sociability and comradeship. Add another figure and the picture is less human – not more so. One is company, two is none. If you wish to symbolise human building draw one dark tower on the horizon; if you wish to symbolise light let there be no star in the sky. Indeed, all through that strangely lit season which we call our day there is but one star in the sky – a large, fierce star which we call the sun. One sun is splendid; six suns would be only vulgar. One Tower Of Giotto is sublime; a row of Towers of Giotto would be only like a row of white posts. The poetry of art is in beholding the single tower; the poetry of nature in seeing the single tree; the poetry of love in following the single woman; the poetry of religion in worshipping the single star. And so, in the same pensive lucidity, I find the poetry of all human anatomy in standing on a single leg. To express complete and perfect leggishness the leg must stand in sublime isolation, like the tower in the wilderness. As Ibsen so finely says, the strongest leg is that which stands most alone.

This lonely leg on which I rest has all the simplicity of some Doric column. The students of architecture tell us that the only legitimate use of a column is to support weight. This column of mine fulfils its legitimate function. It supports weight. Being of an animal and organic consistency, it may even improve by the process, and during these few days that I am thus unequally balanced, the helplessness or dislocation of the one leg may find compensation in the astonishing strength and classic beauty of the other leg. Mrs Mountstuart Jenkinson in Mr George Meredith's novel might pass by at any moment, and seeing me in the stork-like attitude would exclaim, with equal admiration and a more literal exactitude, 'He has a leg.' Notice how this famous literary phrase supports my contention touching this isolation of any admirable thing. Mrs Mountstuart Jenkinson, wishing to make a clear and perfect picture of human grace, said that Sir Willoughby Patterne had a leg. She delicately glossed over and concealed the clumsy and offensive fact that he had really two legs. Two legs were superfluous and irrelevant, a reflection, and a confusion. Two legs would have confused Mrs Mountstuart Jenkinson like two Monuments in London. That having had one good leg he should have another – this would be to use vain repetitions as the Gentiles do. She would have been as much bewildered by him as if he had been a centipede.

All pessimism has a secret optimism for its object. All surrender of life, all denial of pleasure, all darkness, all austerity, all desolation has for its real aim this separation of something so that it may be poignantly and perfectly enjoyed. I feel grateful for the slight sprain which has introduced this mysterious and fascinating division between one of my feet and the other. The way to love anything is to realise that it might be lost. In one of my feet I can feel how strong and splendid a foot is; in the other I can realise how very much otherwise it might have been. The moral of the thing is wholly exhilarating. This world and all our powers in it are far more awful and beautiful than even we know until some accident reminds us. If you wish to perceive that limitless felicity, limit yourself if only for a moment. If you wish to realise how fearfully and wonderfully God's image is made, stand on one leg. If you want to realise the splendid vision of all visible things – wink the other eye.

On Lying in Bed

Lying in bed would be an altogether perfect and supreme experience if only one had a coloured pencil long enough to draw on the ceiling. This, however, is not generally a part of the domestic apparatus on the premises. I think myself that the thing might be managed with several pails of Aspinall and a broom. Only if one worked in a really sweeping and masterly way, and laid on the colour in great washes, it might drip down again on one's face in floods of rich and mingled colour like some strange fairy rain; and that would have its disadvantages. I am afraid it would be necessary to stick to black and white in this form of artistic composition. To that purpose, indeed, the white ceiling would be of the greatest possible use; in fact, it is the only use I think of a white ceiling being put to.

But for the beautiful experiment of lying in bed I might never have discovered it. For years I have been looking for some blank spaces in a modern house to draw on. Paper is much too small for any really allegorical design; as Cyrano de Bergerac says, '*Il me faut des géants.*' But when I tried to find these fine clear spaces in the modern rooms such as we all live in I was continually disappointed. I found an endless pattern and complication of small objects hung like a curtain of fine links between me and my desire.

I examined the walls; I found them to my surprise to be already covered with wallpaper, and I found the wallpaper to be already covered with uninteresting images, all bearing a ridiculous resemblance to each other. I could not understand why one arbitrary symbol (a symbol apparently entirely devoid of any religious or philosophical significance) should thus be sprinkled all over my nice walls like a sort of smallpox. The Bible must be referring to wallpapers, I think, when it says, 'Use not vain repetitions, as the Gentiles do.' Everywhere that I went forlornly, with my pencil or my paint brush, I found that others had unaccountably been before me, spoiling the walls, the curtains, and the furniture with their childish and barbaric designs.

Nowhere did I find a really clear space for sketching until this occasion when I prolonged beyond the proper limit the process of lying on my back in bed. Then the light of that white heaven broke upon my vision, that breadth of mere white which is indeed almost the definition of Paradise, since it means purity and also means freedom. But alas! like all heavens, now that it is seen it is found to be unattainable; it looks more austere and more distant than the blue sky outside the window. For my proposal to paint on it with the bristly end of a broom has been discouraged – never mind by whom; by a person debarred from all political rights – and even my minor proposal to put the other end of the broom into the kitchen fire and turn it to charcoal has not been conceded. Yet I am certain that it was from persons in my position that all the original inspiration came for covering the ceilings of palaces and cathedrals with a riot of fallen angels or victorious gods. I am sure that it was only because Michelangelo was engaged in the ancient and honourable occupation of lying in bed that he ever realised how the roof of the Sistine Chapel might be made into an awful imitation of a divine drama that could only be acted in the heavens.

The tone now commonly taken toward the practice of lying in bed is hypocritical and unhealthy. Of all the marks of modernity that seem to mean a kind of decadence, there is none more menacing and dangerous than the exultation of very small and secondary matters of conduct at the expense of very great and primary ones, at the expense of eternal ties and tragic human morality. If there is one thing worse than the modern weakening of major morals, it is the modern strengthening of minor morals. Thus it is considered more withering to accuse a man of bad taste than of bad ethics. Cleanliness is not next to godliness nowadays, for cleanliness is made essential and godliness is regarded as an offence. A playwright can attack the institution of marriage so long as he does not misrepresent the manners of society, and I have met Ibsenite pessimists who thought it wrong to take beer but right to take prussic acid. Especially this is so in matters of hygiene; notably such matters as lying in bed. Instead of being regarded, as it ought to be, as a matter of personal convenience and adjustment, it has come to be regarded by many as if it were a part of essential morals to get up early in the morning. It is upon the whole part of practical wisdom; but there is nothing good about it or bad about its opposite.

Misers get up early in the morning; and burglars, I am informed, get up the night before. It is the great peril of our society that all its mechanisms may grow more fixed while its spirit grows more fickle. A man's minor actions and arrangements ought to be free, flexible, creative; the things that should be unchangeable are his principles, his ideals. But with us the reverse is true; our views change constantly; but our lunch does not change. Now, I should like men to have strong and rooted conceptions, but as for their lunch, let them have it sometimes in the garden, sometimes in bed, sometimes on the roof, sometimes in the top of a tree. Let them argue from the same first principles, but let them do it in a bed, or a boat, or a balloon. This alarming growth of good habits really means a too great emphasis on those virtues which mere custom can ensure, it means too little emphasis on those virtues which custom can never quite ensure, sudden and splendid virtues of inspired pity or of inspired candour. If ever that abrupt appeal is made to us we may fail. A man can get used to getting up at five o'clock in the morning. A man cannot very well get used to being burnt for his opinions; the first experiment is commonly fatal. Let us pay a little more attention to these possibilities of the heroic and unexpected. I dare say that when I get out of this bed I shall do some deed of an almost terrible virtue.

For those who study the great art of lying in bed there is one emphatic caution to be added. Even for those who can do their work in bed (like journalists), still more for those whose work cannot be done in bed (as, for example, the professional har-pooners of whales), it is obvious that the indulgence must be very occasional. But that is not the caution I mean. The caution is this: if you do lie in bed, be sure you do it without any reason or justification at all. I do not speak, of course, of the seriously sick. But if a healthy man lies in bed, let him do it without a rag of excuse; then he will get up a healthy man. If he does it for some secondary hygienic reason, if he has some scientific explanation, he may get up a hypochondriac.

The Wind and the Trees

I am sitting under tall trees, with a great wind boiling like surf about the tops of them, so that their living load of leaves rocks and roars in something that is at once exultation and agony. I feel, in fact, as if I were actually sitting at the bottom of the sea among mere anchors and ropes, while over my head and over the green twilight of water sounded the everlasting rush of waves and the toil and crash and shipwreck of tremendous ships. The wind tugs at the trees as if it might pluck them root and all out of the earth like tufts of grass. Or, to try yet another desperate figure of speech for this unspeakable energy, the trees are straining and tearing and lashing as if they were a tribe of dragons each tied by the tail.

As I look at these top-heavy giants tortured by an invisible and violent witchcraft, a phrase comes back into my mind. I remember a little boy of my acquaintance who was once walking in Battersea Park under just such torn skies and tossing trees. He did not like the wind at all; it blew in his face too much; it made him shut his eyes; and it blew off his hat, of which he was very proud. He was, as far as I remember, about four. After complaining repeatedly of the atmospheric unrest, he said at last to his mother, 'Well, why don't you take away the trees, and then it wouldn't wind.'

Nothing could be more intelligent or natural than this mistake. Anyone looking for the first time at the trees might fancy that they were indeed vast and titanic fans, which by their mere waving agitated the air around them for miles. Nothing, I say, could be more human and excusable than the belief that it is the trees which make the wind. Indeed, the belief is so human and excusable that it is, as a matter of fact, the belief of about ninety-nine out of a hundred of the philosophers, reformers, sociologists, and politicians of the great age in which we live. My small friend was, in fact, very like the principal modern thinkers; only much nicer.

In the little apologue or parable which he has thus the honour of inventing, the trees stand for all visible things and the wind for the invisible. The wind is the spirit which bloweth where it listeth; the trees are the material things of the world which are blown where the spirit lists. The wind is philosophy, religion, revolution; the trees are cities and civilisations. We only know that there is a wind because the trees on some distant hill suddenly go mad. We only know that there is a real revolution because all the chimney-pots go mad on the whole skyline of the city.

Just as the ragged outline of a tree grows suddenly more ragged and rises into fantastic crests or tattered tails, so the human city rises under the wind of the spirit into toppling temples or sudden spires. No man has ever seen a revolution. Mobs pouring through the palaces, blood pouring down the gutters, the guillotine lifted higher than the throne, a prison in ruins, a people in arms – these things are not revolution, but the results of revolution.

You cannot see a wind; you can only see that there is a wind. So, also, you cannot see a revolution; you can only see that there is a revolution. And there never has been in the history of the world a real revolution, brutally active and decisive, which was not preceded by unrest and new dogma in the reign of invisible things. All revolutions began by being abstract. Most revolutions began by being quite pedantically abstract.

The wind is up above the world before a twig on the tree has moved. So there must always be a battle in the sky before there is a battle on the earth. Since it is lawful to pray for the coming of the kingdom, it is lawful also to pray for the coming of the revolution that shall restore the kingdom. It is lawful to hope to hear the wind of Heaven in the trees. It is lawful to pray 'Thine anger come on earth as it is in Heaven.'

The great human dogma, then, is that the wind moves the trees. The great human heresy is that the trees move the wind. When people begin to say that the material circumstances have alone created the moral circumstances, then they have prevented all possibility of serious change. For if my circumstances have made me wholly stupid, how can I be certain even that I am right in altering those circumstances?

The man who represents all thought as an accident of environment is simply smashing and discrediting all his own thoughts – including that one. To treat the human mind as having an ultimate authority is necessary to any kind of thinking, even free thinking. And nothing will ever be reformed in this age or country unless we realise that the moral fact comes first.

For example, most of us, I suppose, have seen in print and heard in debating clubs an endless discussion that goes on between socialists and total abstainers. The latter say that drink leads to poverty; the former say that poverty leads to drink. I can only wonder at their either of them being content with such simple physical explanations. Surely it is obvious that the thing which among the English proletariat leads to poverty is the same as the thing which leads to drink; the absence of strong civic dignity, the absence of an instinct that resists degradation.

When you have discovered why enormous English estates were not long ago cut up into small holdings like the land of France, you will have discovered why the Englishman is more drunken than the Frenchman. The Englishman, among his million delightful virtues, really has this quality, which may strictly be called 'hand to mouth', because under its influence a man's hand automatically seeks his own mouth, instead of seeking (as it sometimes should do) his oppressor's nose. And a man who says that the English inequality in land is due only to economic causes, or that the drunkenness of England is due only to economic causes, is saying something so absurd that he cannot really have thought what he was saying.

Yet things quite as preposterous as this are said and written under the influence of that great spectacle of babyish helplessness, the economic theory of history. We have people who represent that all great historic motives were economic, and then have to howl at the top of their voices in order to induce the modern democracy to act on economic motives. The extreme Marxian politicians in England exhibit themselves as a small, heroic minority, trying vainly to induce the world to do what, according to their theory, the world always does. The truth is, of course, that there will be a social revolution the moment the thing has ceased to be purely economic. You can never have a revolution in order to establish a democracy. You must have a democracy in order to have a revolution.

I get up from under the trees, for the wind and the slight rain have ceased. The trees stand up like golden pillars in a clear sunlight. The tossing of the trees and the blowing of the wind have ceased simultaneously. So I suppose there are still modern philosophers who will maintain that the trees make the wind.

The Dickensian

He was a quiet man, dressed in dark clothes, with a large limp straw hat; with something almost military in his moustache and whiskers, but with a quite unmilitary stoop and very dreamy eyes. He was gazing with a rather gloomy interest at the cluster, one might almost say the tangle, of small shipping which grew thicker as our little pleasure boat crawled up into Yarmouth Harbour. A boat entering this harbour, as every one knows, does not enter in front of the town like a foreigner, but creeps round at the back like a traitor taking the town in the rear. The passage of the river seems almost too narrow for traffic, and in consequence the bigger ships look colossal. As we passed under a timber ship from Norway, which seemed to block up the heavens like a cathedral, the man in a straw hat pointed to an odd wooden figurehead carved like a woman, and said, like one continuing a conversation, 'Now, why have they left off having them? They didn't do anyone any harm.'

I replied with some flippancy about the captain's wife being jealous; but I knew in my heart that the man had struck a deep note. There has been something in our most recent civilisation which is mysteriously hostile to such healthy and humane symbols.

'They hate anything like that, which is human and pretty,' he continued, exactly echoing my thoughts. 'I believe they broke up all the jolly old figureheads with hatchets and enjoyed doing it.'

'Like Mr Quilp,' I answered, 'when he battered the wooden Admiral with the poker.'

His whole face suddenly became alive, and for the first time he stood erect and stared at me.

'Do you come to Yarmouth for that?' he asked.

'For what?'

'For Dickens,' he answered, and drummed with his foot on the deck.

'No,' I answered; 'I come for fun, though that is much the same thing.'

'I always come,' he answered quietly, 'to find Peggotty's boat. It isn't here.'

And when he said that I understood him perfectly.

There are two Yarmouths; I daresay there are two hundred to the people who live there. I myself have never come to the end of the list of Batterseas. But there are two to the stranger and tourist; the poor part, which is dignified, and the prosperous part, which is savagely vulgar. My new friend haunted the first of these like a ghost; to the latter he would only distantly allude.

'The place is very much spoilt now... trippers, you know,' he would say, not at all scornfully, but simply sadly. That was the nearest he would go to an admission of the monstrous watering place that lay along the front, outblazing the sun, and more deafening than the sea. But behind – out of earshot of this uproar – there are lanes so narrow that they seem like secret entrances to some hidden place of repose. There are squares so brimful of silence that to plunge into one of them is like plunging into a pool. In these places the man and I paced up and down talking about Dickens, or, rather, doing what all true Dickensians do, telling each other verbatim long passages which both of us knew quite well already. We were really in the atmosphere of the older England. Fishermen passed us who might well have been characters like Peggotty; we went into a musty curiosity shop and bought pipe-stoppers carved into figures from Pickwick. The evening was settling down between all the buildings with that slow gold that seems to soak everything when we went into the church.

In the growing darkness of the church, my eye caught the coloured windows which on that clear golden evening were flaming with all the passionate heraldry of the most fierce and ecstatic of Christian arts. At length I said to my companion:

'Do you see that angel over there? I think it must be meant for the angel at the sepulchre.'

He saw that I was somewhat singularly moved, and he raised his eyebrows.

'I daresay,' he said. 'What is there odd about that?'

After a pause I said, 'Do you remember what the angel at the sepulchre said?'

'Not particularly,' he answered; 'but where are you off to in such a hurry?'

I walked him rapidly out of the still square, past the fishermen's almshouses, towards the coast, he still inquiring indignantly where I was going.

'I am going,' I said, 'to put pennies in automatic machines on the beach. I am going to have my photograph taken. I am going to drink ginger beer out of its original bottle. I will buy some picture postcards. I do want a boat. I am ready to listen to a concertina, and but for the defects of my education should be ready to play it. I am willing to ride on a donkey; that is, if the donkey is willing. I am willing to be a donkey; for all this was commanded me by the angel in the stained-glass window.'

'I really think,' said the Dickensian, 'that I had better put you in charge of your relations.'

'Sir,' I answered, 'there are certain writers to whom humanity owes much, whose talent is yet of so shy or delicate or retrospective a type that we do well to link it with certain quaint places or certain perishing associations. It would not be unnatural to look for the spirit of Horace Walpole at Strawberry Hill, or even for the shade of Thackeray in Old Kensington. But let us have no antiquarianism about Dickens, for Dickens is not an antiquity. Dickens looks not backward, but forward; he might look at our modern mobs with satire, or with fury, but he would love to look at them. He might lash our democracy, but it would be because, like a democrat, he asked much from it.

We will not have all his books bound up under the title of 'The Old Curiosity Shop'. Rather we will have them all bound up under the title of 'Great Expectations'. Wherever humanity is he would have us face it and make something of it, swallow it with a holy cannibalism, and assimilate it with the digestion of a giant. We must take these trippers as he would have taken them, and tear out of them their tragedy and their farce. Do you remember now what the angel said at the sepulchre? "Why seek ye the living among the dead? He is not here; he is risen.'"

With that we came out suddenly on the wide stretch of the sands, which were black with the knobs and masses of our laughing and quite desperate democracy. And the sunset, which was now in its final glory, flung far over all of them a red flush and glitter like the gigantic firelight of Dickens. In that strange evening light every figure looked at once grotesque and attractive, as if he had a story to tell. I heard a little girl (who was being throttled by another little girl) say by way of self-vindication, 'My sister-in-law 'as got four rings aside her weddin' ring!'

I stood and listened for more, but my friend went away.

In Topsy-Turvy Land

Last week, in an idle metaphor, I took the tumbling of trees and the secret energy of the wind as typical of the visible world moving under the violence of the invisible. I took this metaphor merely because I happened to be writing the article in a wood. Nevertheless, now that I return to Fleet Street (which seems to me, I confess, much better and more poetical than all the wild woods in the world), I am strangely haunted by this accidental comparison. The people's figures seem a forest and their soul a wind. All the human personalities which speak or signal to me seem to have this fantastic character of the fringe of the forest against the sky. That man that talks to me, what is he but an articulate tree? That driver of a van who waves his hands wildly at me to tell me to get out of the way, what is he but a bunch of branches stirred and swayed by a spiritual wind, a sylvan object that I can continue to contemplate with calm? That policeman who lifts his hand to warn three omnibuses of the peril that they run in encountering my person, what is he but a shrub shaken for a moment with that blast of human law which is a thing stronger than anarchy? Gradually this impression of the woods wears off. But this black-and-white contrast between the visible and invisible, this deep sense that the one essential belief is belief in the invisible as against the visible, is suddenly and sensationally brought back to my mind. Exactly at the moment when Fleet Street has grown most familiar (that is, most bewildering and bright), my eye catches a poster of vivid violet, on which I see written in large black letters these remarkable words: 'Should Shop Assistants Marry?'

When I saw those words everything might just as well have turned upside down. The men in Fleet Street might have been walking about on their hands. The cross of St Paul's might have been hanging in the air upside down. For I realise that I have really come into a topsy-turvy country; I have come into the country where men do definitely believe that the waving of the trees makes the wind. That is to say, they believe that the material circumstances, however black and twisted, are more important than the spiritual realities, however powerful and pure. 'Should Shop Assistants Marry?' I am puzzled to think what some periods and schools of human history would have made of such a question. The ascetics of the East or of some periods of the early Church would have thought that the question meant, 'Are not shop assistants too saintly, too much of another world, even to feel the emotions of the sexes?' But I suppose that is not what the purple poster means. In some pagan cities it might have meant, 'Shall slaves so vile as shop assistants even be allowed to propagate their abject race?' But I suppose that is not what the purple poster meant. We must face, I fear, the full insanity of what it does mean. It does really mean that a section of the human race is asking whether the primary relations of the two human sexes are particularly good for modern shops. The human race is asking whether Adam and Eve are entirely suitable for Marshall and Snelgrove. If this is not topsy-turvy I cannot imagine what would be. We ask whether the universal institution will improve our (please God) temporary institution. Yet I have known many such questions. For instance, I have known a man ask seriously, 'Does Democracy help the Empire?' Which is like saying, 'Is art favourable to frescoes?'

I say that there are many such questions asked. But if the world ever runs short of them, I can suggest a large number of questions of precisely the same kind, based on precisely the same principle.

'Do Feet Improve Boots?' 'Is Bread Better when Eaten?' 'Should Hats have Heads in them?' 'Do People Spoil a Town?' 'Do Walls Ruin Wallpapers?' 'Should Neckties Enclose Necks?' 'Do Hands Hurt Walking Sticks?' 'Does Burning Destroy Firewood?' 'Is Cleanliness Good for Soap?' 'Can Cricket Really Improve Cricket Bats?' 'Shall We Take Brides with our Wedding Rings?' and a hundred others.

Not one of these questions differs at all in intellectual purport or in intellectual value from the question which I have quoted from the purple poster, or from any of the typical questions asked by half of the earnest economists of our times. All the questions they ask are of this character; they are all tinged with this same initial absurdity. They do not ask if the means is suited to the end; they all ask (with profound and penetrating scepticism) if the end is suited to the means. They do not ask whether the tail suits the dog. They all ask whether a dog is (by the highest artistic canons) the most ornamental appendage that can be put at the end of a tail. In short, instead of asking whether our modern arrangements, our streets, trades, bargains, laws, and concrete institutions are suited to the primal and permanent idea of a healthy human life, they never admit that healthy human life into the discussion at all, except suddenly and accidentally at odd moments; and then they only ask whether that healthy human life is suited to our streets and trades. Perfection may be attainable or unattainable as an end. It may or may not be possible to talk of imperfection as a means to perfection. But surely it passes toleration to talk of perfection as a means to imperfection. The New Jerusalem may be a reality. It may be a dream. But surely it is too outrageous to say that the New Jerusalem is a reality on the road to Birmingham.

This is the most enormous and at the same time the most secret of the modern tyrannies of materialism. In theory the thing ought to be simple enough. A really human human being would always put the spiritual things first. A walking and speaking statue of God finds himself at one particular moment employed as a shop assistant. He has in himself a power of terrible love, a promise of paternity, a thirst for some loyalty that shall unify life, and in the ordinary course of things he asks himself, 'How far do the existing conditions of those assisting in shops fit in with my evident and epic destiny in the matter of love and marriage?' But here, as I have said, comes in the quiet and crushing power of modern materialism. It prevents him

45

rising in rebellion, as he would otherwise do. By perpetually talking about environment and visible things, by perpetually talking about economics and physical necessity, painting and keeping repainted a perpetual picture of iron machinery and merciless engines, of rails of steel, and of towers of stone, modern materialism at last produces this tremendous impression in which the truth is stated upside down. At last the result is achieved. The man does not say as he ought to have said, 'Should married men endure being modern shop assistants?' The man says, 'Should shop assistants marry?' Triumph has completed the immense illusion of materialism. The slave does not say, 'Are these chains worthy of me?' The slave says scientifically and contentedly, 'Am I even worthy of these chains?'

What I Found in My Pocket

Once when I was very young I met one of those men who have made the Empire what it is – a man in an astracan coat, with an astracan moustache – a tight, black, curly moustache. Whether he put on the moustache with the coat or whether his Napoleonic will enabled him not only to grow a moustache in the usual place, but also to grow little moustaches all over his clothes, I do not know. I only remember that he said to me the following words: 'A man can't get on nowadays by hanging about with his hands in his pockets.' I made reply with the quite obvious flippancy that perhaps a man got on by having his hands in other people's pockets; whereupon he began to argue about Moral Evolution, so I suppose what I said had some truth in it. But the incident now comes back to me, and connects itself with another incident – if you can call it an incident – which happened to me only the other day.

I have only once in my life picked a pocket, and then (perhaps through some absent-mindedness) I picked my own. My act can really with some reason be so described. For in taking things out of my own pocket I had at least one of the more tense and quivering emotions of the thief; I had a complete ignorance and a profound curiosity as to what I should find there. Perhaps it would be the exaggeration of eulogy to call me a tidy person. But I can always pretty satisfactorily account for all my possessions. I can always tell where they are, and what I have done with them, so long as I can keep them out of my pockets. If once anything slips into those unknown abysses, I wave it a sad Virgilian farewell. I suppose that the things that I have dropped into my pockets are still there; the same presumption applies to the things that I have dropped into the sea. But I regard the riches stored in both these bottomless chasms with the same reverent ignorance. They tell us that on the last day the sea will give up its dead; and I suppose that on the same occasion long strings of extraordinary things will come running out of my pockets. But I have quite forgotten what any of them are; and there is really nothing (excepting the money) that I shall be at all surprised at finding among them.

Such at least has hitherto been my state of innocence. I here only wish briefly to recall the special, extraordinary, and hitherto unprecedented circumstances which led me in cold blood, and being of sound mind, to turn out my pockets. I was locked up in a third-class carriage for a rather long journey. The time was towards evening, but it might have been anything, for everything resembling earth or sky or light or shade was painted out as if with a great wet brush by an unshifting sheet of quite colourless rain. I had no books or newspapers. I had not even a pencil and a scrap of paper with which to write a religious epic. There were no advertisements on the walls of the carriage, otherwise I could have plunged into the study, for any collection of printed words is quite enough to suggest infinite complexities of mental ingenuity. When I find myself opposite the words 'Sunlight Soap' I can exhaust all the aspects of Sun Worship, Apollo, and Summer poetry before I go on to the less congenial subject of soap. But there was no printed word or picture anywhere; there was nothing but blank wood inside the carriage and blank wet without. Now I deny most energetically that anything is, or can be, uninteresting. So I stared at the joints of the walls and seats, and began thinking hard on the fascinating subject of wood. Just as I had begun to realise why, perhaps, it was that Christ was a carpenter, rather than a bricklayer, or a baker, or anything else, I suddenly started upright, and remembered my pockets. I was carrying about with me an unknown treasury. I had a British Museum and a South Kensington collection of unknown curios hung all over me in different places. I began to take the things out.

The first thing I came upon consisted of piles and heaps of Battersea tram tickets. There were enough to equip a paper chase. They shook down in showers like confetti. Primarily, of course, they touched my patriotic emotions, and brought tears to my eyes; also they provided me with the printed matter I required, for I found on the back of them some short but striking little scientific essays about some kind of pill. Comparatively speaking, in my then destitution, those tickets might be regarded as a small but well-chosen scientific library. Should my railway journey continue (which seemed likely at the time) for a few months longer, I could imagine myself throwing myself into the controversial aspects of the pill, composing replies and rejoinders pro and con upon the data furnished to me. But after all it was the symbolic quality of the tickets that moved me most. For as certainly as the cross of St George means English patriotism, those scraps of paper meant all that municipal patriotism which is now, perhaps, the greatest hope of England.

The next thing that I took out was a pocket knife. A pocket knife, I need hardly say, would require a thick book full of moral meditations all to itself. A knife typifies one of the most primary of those practical origins upon which as upon low, thick pillows all our human civilisation reposes. Metals, the mystery of the thing called iron and of the thing called steel, led me off half-dazed into a kind of dream. I saw into the intrails of dim, damp wood, where the first man among all the common stones found the strange stone. I saw a vague and violent battle, in which stone axes broke and stone knives were splintered against something shining and new in the hand of one desperate man. I heard all the hammers on all the anvils of the earth. I saw all the swords of Feudal and all the weals of Industrial war. For the knife is only a short sword; and the pocket knife is a secret sword. I opened it and looked at that brilliant and terrible tongue which we call a blade; and I thought that perhaps it was the symbol of the oldest of the needs of man. The next moment I knew that I was wrong; for the thing that came next out of my pocket was a box of matches. Then I saw fire, which is stronger even than steel, the old, fierce female thing, the thing we all love, but dare not touch.

The next thing I found was a piece of chalk; and I saw in it all the art and all the frescoes of the world. The next was a coin of a very modest value; and I saw in it not only the image and superscription of our own Caesar, but all government and order since the world began. But I have not space to say what were the items in the long and splendid procession of poetical symbols that came pouring out. I cannot tell you all the things that were in my pocket. I can tell you one thing, however, that I could not find in my pocket. I allude to my railway ticket.

The Dragon's Grandmother

I met a man the other day who did not believe in fairy tales. I do not mean that he did not believe in the incidents narrated in them – that he did not believe that a pumpkin could turn into a coach. He did, indeed, entertain this curious disbelief. And, like all the other people I have ever met who entertained it, he was wholly unable to give me an intelligent reason for it. He tried the laws of nature, but he soon dropped that. Then he said that pumpkins were unalterable in ordinary experience, and that we all reckoned on their infinitely protracted pumpkinity. But I pointed out to him that this was not an attitude we adopt specially towards impossible marvels, but simply the attitude we adopt towards all unusual occurrences. If we were certain of miracles we should not count on them. Things that happen very seldom we all leave out of our calculations, whether they are miraculous or not. I do not expect a glass of water to be turned into wine; but neither do I expect a glass of water to be poisoned with prussic acid. I do not in ordinary business relations act on the assumption that the editor is a fairy; but neither do I act on the assumption that he is a Russian spy, or the lost heir of the Holy Roman Empire. What we assume in action is not that the natural order is unalterable, but simply that it is much safer to bet on uncommon incidents than on common ones. This does not touch the credibility of any attested tale about a Russian spy or a pumpkin turned into a coach. If I had seen a pumpkin turned into a Panhard motor car with my own eyes that would not make me any more inclined to assume that the same thing would happen again. I should not invest largely in pumpkins with an eye to the motor trade. Cinderella got a ball dress from the fairy; but I do not suppose that she looked after her own clothes any the less after it.

But the view that fairy tales cannot really have happened, though crazy, is common. The man I speak of disbelieved in fairy tales in an even more amazing and perverted sense. He actually thought that fairy tales ought not to be told to children. That is (like a belief in slavery or annexation) one of those intellectual errors which lie very near to ordinary mortal sins. There are some refusals which, though they may be done what is called conscientiously, yet carry so much of their whole horror in the very act of them, that a man must in doing them not only harden but slightly corrupt his heart. One of them was the refusal of milk to young mothers when their husbands were in the field against us. Another is the refusal of fairy tales to children.

The man had come to see me in connection with some silly society of which I am an enthusiastic member; he was a fresh-coloured, short-sighted young man, like a stray curate who was too helpless even to find his way to the Church of England. He had a curious green necktie and a very long neck; I am always meeting idealists with very long necks. Perhaps it is that their eternal aspiration slowly lifts their heads nearer and nearer to the stars. Or perhaps it has something to do with the fact that so many of them are vegetarians: perhaps they are slowly evolving the neck of the giraffe so that they can eat all the tops of the trees in Kensington Gardens. These things are in every sense above me. Such, anyhow, was the young man who did not believe in fairy tales; and by a curious coincidence he entered the room when I had just finished looking through a pile of contemporary fiction, and had begun to read *Grimm's Fairy Tales* as a natural consequence.

The modern novels stood before me, however, in a stack; and you can imagine their titles for yourself. There was *Suburban Sue: A Tale of Psychology*, and also *Psychological Sue: A Tale of Suburbia*; there was *Trixy: A Temperament*, and *Man-Hate: A Monochrome*, and all those nice things. I read them with real interest, but, curiously enough, I grew tired of them at last, and when I saw *Grimm's Fairy Tales* lying accidentally on the table, I gave a cry of indecent joy. Here at least, here at last, one could find a little common sense. I opened the book, and my eyes fell on these splendid and satisfying words, 'The Dragon's Grand-mother'. That at least was reasonable; that at least was true. 'The Dragon's Grandmother'! While I was rolling this first touch of ordinary human reality upon my tongue, I looked up suddenly and saw this monster with a green tie standing in the doorway.

I listened to what he said about the society politely enough, I hope; but when he incidentally mentioned that he did not believe in fairy tales, I broke out beyond control. 'Man,' I said, 'who are you that you should not believe in fairy tales? It is much easier to believe in Blue Beard than to believe in you. A blue beard is a misfortune; but there are green ties which are sins. It is far easier to believe in a million fairy tales than to believe in one man who does not like fairy tales. I would rather kiss Grimm instead of a Bible and swear to all his stories as if they were thirty-nine articles than say seriously and out of my heart that there can be such a man as you; that you are not some temptation of the devil or some delusion from the void. Look at these plain, homely, practical words. "The Dragon's Grand-mother", that is all right; that is rational almost to the verge of rationalism. If there was a dragon, he had a grandmother. But you – you had no grandmother! If you had known one, she would have taught you to love fairy tales.

'You had no father, you had no mother; no natural causes can explain you. You cannot be. I believe many things which I have not seen; but of such things as you it may be said, "Blessed is he that has seen and yet has disbelieved".'

It seemed to me that he did not follow me with sufficient delicacy, so I moderated my tone. 'Can you not see,' I said, 'that fairy tales in their essence are quite solid and straightforward; but that this everlasting fiction about modern life is in its nature essentially incredible? Folklore means that the soul is sane, but that the universe is wild and full of marvels. Realism means that the world is dull and full of routine, but that the soul is sick and screaming. The problem of the fairy tale is – what will a healthy man do with a fantastic world? The problem of the modern novel is – what will a madman do with a dull world? In the fairy tales the cosmos goes mad; but the hero does not go mad.

'In the modern novels the hero is mad before the book begins, and suffers from the harsh steadiness and cruel sanity of the cosmos. In the excellent tale of "The Dragon's Grandmother", in all the other tales of Grimm, it is assumed that the young man setting out on his travels will have all substantial truths in him; that he will be brave, full of faith, reasonable, that he will respect his parents, keep his word, rescue one kind of people, defy another kind, *parcere subjectis et debellare*, etc. Then, having assumed this centre of sanity, the writer entertains himself by fancying what would happen if the whole world went mad all round it, if the sun turned green and the moon blue, if horses had six legs and giants had two heads. But your modern literature takes insanity as its centre. Therefore, it loses the interest even of insanity. A lunatic is not startling to himself, because he is quite serious; that is what makes him a lunatic. A man who thinks he is a piece of glass is to himself as dull as a piece of glass. A man who thinks he is a chicken is to himself as common as a chicken. It is only sanity that can see even a wild poetry in insanity. Therefore, these wise old tales made the hero ordinary and the tale extraordinary. But you have made the hero extraordinary and the tale ordinary – so ordinary – oh, so very ordinary.'

I saw him still gazing at me fixedly. Some nerve snapped in me under the hypnotic stare. I leapt to my feet and cried, 'In the name of God and Democracy and the Dragon's grandmother – in the name of all good things – I charge you to avaunt and haunt this house no more.' Whether or no it was the result of the exorcism, there is no doubt that he definitely went away.

The Red Angel

I find that there really are human beings who think fairy tales bad for children. I do not speak of the man in the green tie, for him I can never count truly human. But a lady has written me an earnest letter saying that fairy tales ought not to be taught to children even if they are true. She says that it is cruel to tell children fairy tales, because it frightens them. You might just as well say that it is cruel to give girls sentimental novels because it makes them cry. All this kind of talk is based on that complete forgetting of what a child is like which has been the firm foundation of so many educational schemes. If you kept bogies and goblins away from children they would make them up for themselves. One small child in the dark can invent more hells than Swedenborg. One small child can imagine monsters too big and black to get into any picture, and give them names too unearthly and cacophonous to have occurred in the cries of any lunatic. The child, to begin with, commonly likes horrors, and he continues to indulge in them even when he does not like them. There is just as much difficulty in saying exactly where pure pain begins in his case, as there is in ours when we walk of our own free will into the torture-chamber of a great tragedy. The fear does not come from fairy tales; the fear comes from the universe of the soul.

The timidity of the child or the savage is entirely reasonable; they are alarmed at this world, because this world is a very alarming place. They dislike being alone because it is verily and indeed an awful idea to be alone. Barbarians fear the unknown for the same reason that Agnostics worship it – because it is a fact. Fairy tales, then, are not responsible for producing in children fear, or any of the shapes of fear; fairy tales do not give the child the idea of the evil or the ugly; that is in the child already, because it is in the world already. Fairy tales do not give the child his first idea of bogey. What fairy tales give the child is his first clear idea of the possible defeat of bogey. The baby has known the dragon intimately ever since he had an imagination. What the fairy tale provides for him is a St George to kill the dragon.

Exactly what the fairy tale does is this: it accustoms him for a series of clear pictures to the idea that these limitless terrors had a limit, that these shapeless enemies have enemies in the knights of God, that there is something in the universe more mystical than darkness, and stronger than strong fear. When I was a child I have stared at the darkness until the whole black bulk of it turned into one giant taller than heaven. If there was one star in the sky it only made him a Cyclops. But fairy tales restored my mental health, for next day I read an authentic account of how a giant with one eye, of quite equal dimensions, had been baffled by a little boy like myself (of similar inexperience and even lower social status) by means of a sword, some bad riddles, and a brave heart. Sometimes the sea at night seemed as dreadful as any dragon. But then I was acquainted with many youngest sons and little sailors to whom a dragon or two was as simple as the sea.

Take the most horrible of Grimm's tales in incident and imagery, the excellent tale of the 'Boy who Could not Shudder', and you will see what I mean. There are some living shocks in that tale. I remember specially a man's legs which fell down the chimney by themselves and walked about the room, until they were rejoined by the severed head and body which fell down the chimney after them. That is very good. But the point of the story and the point of the reader's feelings is not that these things are frightening, but the far more striking fact that the hero was not frightened at them. The most fearful of all these fearful wonders was his own absence of fear. He slapped the bogies on the back and asked the devils to drink wine with him; many a time in my youth, when stifled with some modern morbidity, I have prayed for a double portion of his spirit. If you have not read the end of his story, go and read it; it is the wisest thing in the world. The hero was at last taught to shudder by taking a wife, who threw a pail of cold water over him. In that one sentence there is more of the real meaning of marriage than in all the books about sex that cover Europe and America.

At the four corners of a child's bed stand Perseus and Roland, Sigurd and St George. If you withdraw the guard of heroes you are not making him rational; you are only leaving him to fight the devils alone. For the devils, alas, we have always believed in. The hopeful element in the universe has in modern times continually been denied and reasserted; but the hopeless element has never for a moment been denied. As I told 'H.N.B.' (whom I pause to wish a Happy Christmas in its most superstitious sense), the one thing modern people really do believe in is damnation. The greatest of purely modern poets summed up the really modern attitude in that fine Agnostic line –

There may be Heaven; there must be Hell.

The gloomy view of the universe has been a continuous tradition; and the new types of spiritual investigation or conjecture all begin by being gloomy. A little while ago men believed in no spirits. Now they are beginning rather slowly to believe in rather slow spirits.

Some people objected to spiritualism, table rappings, and such things, because they were undignified, because the ghosts cracked jokes or waltzed with dinner tables. I do not share this objection in the least. I wish the spirits were more farcical than they are. That they should make more jokes and better ones, would be my suggestion. For almost all the spiritualism of our time, in so far as it is new, is solemn and sad. Some Pagan gods were lawless, and some Christian saints were a little too serious; but the spirits of modern spiritualism are both lawless and serious – a disgusting combination. The specially contemporary spirits are not only devils, they are blue devils. This is, first and last, the real value of Christmas; in so far as the mythology remains at all it is a kind of happy mythology. Personally, of course, I believe in Santa Claus; but it is the season of forgiveness, and I will forgive others for not doing so. But if there is anyone who does not comprehend the defect in our world which I am civilising, I should recommend him, for instance, to read a story by Mr Henry James, called *The Turn of the Screw*. It is one of the most powerful things ever written, and it is one of the things about which I doubt most whether it ought ever to have been written at all. It describes two innocent children gradually growing at once omniscient and half-witted under the influence of the foul ghosts of a groom and a governess. As I say, I doubt whether Mr Henry James ought to have published it (no, it is not indecent, do not buy it; it is a spiritual matter), but I think the question so doubtful that I will give that truly great man a chance. I will approve the thing as well as admire it if he will write another tale just as powerful about two children and Santa Claus. If he will not, or cannot, then the conclusion is clear; we can deal strongly with gloomy mystery, but not with happy mystery; we are not rationalists, but diabolists.

I have thought vaguely of all this staring at a great red fire that stands up in the room like a great red angel. But, perhaps, you have never heard of a red angel. But you have heard of a blue devil. That is exactly what I mean.

A Great Man

People accuse journalism of being too personal; but to me it has always seemed far too impersonal. It is charged with tearing away the veils from private life; but it seems to me to be always dropping diaphanous but blinding veils between men and men. The Yellow Press is abused for exposing facts which are private; I wish the Yellow Press did anything so valuable. It is exactly the decisive individual touches that it never gives; and a proof of this is that after one has met a man a million times in the newspapers it is always a complete shock and reversal to meet him in real life. The Yellow Pressman seems to have no power of catching the first fresh fact about a man that dominates all after impressions. For instance, before I met Bernard Shaw I heard that he spoke with a reckless desire for paradox or a sneering hatred of sentiment; but I never knew till he opened his mouth that he spoke with an Irish accent, which is more important than all the other criticisms put together.

Journalism is not personal enough. So far from digging out private personalities, it cannot even report the obvious personalities on the surface. Now there is one vivid and even bodily impression of this kind which we have all felt when we met great poets or politicians, but which never finds its way into the newspapers. I mean the impression that they are much older than we thought they were. We connect great men with their great triumphs, which generally happened some years ago, and many recruits enthusiastic for the thin Napoleon of Marengo must have found themselves in the presence of the fat Napoleon of Leipzic.

I remember reading a newspaper account of how a certain rising politician confronted the House of Lords with the enthusiasm almost of boyhood. It described how his 'brave young voice' rang in the rafters. I also remember that I met him some days after, and he was considerably older than my own father.

I mention this truth for only one purpose: all this generalisation leads up to only one fact – the fact that I once met a great man who was younger than I expected.

I had come over the wooded wall from the villages about Epsom, and down a stumbling path between trees towards the valley in which Dorking lies. A warm sunlight was working its way through the leafage; a sunlight which though of saintless gold had taken on the quality of evening. It was such sunlight as reminds a man that the sun begins to set an instant after noon. It seemed to lessen as the wood strengthened and the road sank.

I had a sensation peculiar to such entangled descents; I felt that the treetops that closed above me were the fixed and real things, certain as the level of the sea; but that the solid earth was every instant failing under my feet. In a little while that splendid sunlight showed only in splashes, like flaming stars and suns in the dome of green sky. Around me in that emerald twilight were trunks of trees of every plain or twisted type; it was like a chapel supported on columns of every earthly and unearthly style of architecture.

Without intention my mind grew full of fancies on the nature of the forest; on the whole philosophy of mystery and force. For the meaning of woods is the combination of energy with complexity. A forest is not in the least rude or barbarous; it is only dense with delicacy. Unique shapes that an artist would copy or a philosopher watch for years if he found them in an open plain are here mingled and confounded; but it is not a darkness of deformity. It is a darkness of life; a darkness of perfection. And I began to think how much of the highest human obscurity is like this, and how much men have misunderstood it. People will tell you, for instance, that theology became elaborate because it was dead. Believe me, if it had been dead it would never have become elaborate; it is only the live tree that grows too many branches.

These trees thinned and fell away from each other, and I came out into deep grass and a road. I remember being surprised that the evening was so far advanced; I had a fancy that this valley had a sunset all to itself. I went along that road according to directions that had been given me, and passed the gateway in a slight paling beyond which the wood changed only faintly to a garden. It was as if the curious courtesy and fineness of that character I was to meet went out from him upon the valley; for I felt on all these things the finger of that quality which the old English called 'faërie'; it is the quality which those can never understand who think of the past as merely brutal; it is an ancient elegance such as there is in trees. I went through the garden and saw an old man sitting by a table, looking small-ish in his big chair. He was already an invalid, and his hair and beard were both white; not like snow, for snow is cold and heavy, but like something feathery, or even fierce; rather they were white like the white thistledown. I came up quite close to him; he looked at me as he put out his frail hand, and I saw of a sudden that his eyes were startlingly young. He was the one great man of the old world whom I have met who was not a mere statue over his own grave.

He was deaf and he talked like a torrent. He did not talk about the books he had written; he was far too much alive for that. He talked about the books he had not written. He un-rolled a purple bundle of romances which he had never had time to sell. He asked me to write one of the stories for him, as he would have asked the milkman, if he had been talking to the milkman. It was a splendid and frantic story, a sort of astronomical farce. It was all about a man who was rushing up to the Royal Society with the only possible way of avoiding an earth-destroying comet; and it showed how, even on this huge errand, the man was tripped up at every other minute by his own weakness and vanities; how he lost a train by trifling or was put in gaol for brawling. That is only one of them; there were ten or twenty more. Another, I dimly remember, was a version of the fall of Parnell; the idea that a quite honest man might be secret from a pure love of secrecy, of solitary self-control.

I went out of that garden with a blurred sensation of the million possibilities of creative literature. The feeling increased as my way fell back into the wood; for a wood is a palace with a million corridors that cross each other everywhere. I really had the feeling that I had seen the creative quality; which is supernatural. I had seen what Virgil calls the Old Man of the Forest: I had seen an elf. The trees thronged behind my path; I have never seen him again; and now I shall not see him, because he died last Tuesday.

The Toy Theatre

There is only one reason why all grown-up people do not play with toys; and it is a fair reason. The reason is that playing with toys takes so very much more time and trouble than anything else. Playing as children mean playing is the most serious thing in the world; and as soon as we have small duties or small sorrows we have to abandon to some extent so enormous and ambitious a plan of life. We have enough strength for politics and commerce and art and philosophy; we have not enough strength for play. This is a truth which every one will recognise who, as a child, has ever played with anything at all; any one who has played with bricks, any one who has played with dolls, any one who has played with tin soldiers. My journalistic work, which earns money, is not pursued with such awful persistency as that work which earned nothing.

Take the case of bricks. If you publish a book tomorrow in twelve volumes (it would be just like you) on 'The Theory and Practice of European Architecture', your work may be laborious, but it is fundamentally frivolous. It is not serious as the work of a child piling one brick on the other is serious; for the simple reason that if your book is a bad book no one will ever be able ultimately and entirely to prove to you that it is a bad book. Whereas if his balance of bricks is a bad balance of bricks, it will simply tumble down. And if I know anything of children, he will set to work solemnly and sadly to build it up again. Whereas, if I know anything of authors, nothing would induce you to write your book again, or even to think of it again if you could help it.

Take the case of dolls. It is much easier to care for an educational cause than to care for a doll. It is as easy to write an article on education as to write an article on toffee or tramcars or anything else. But it is almost as difficult to look after a doll as to look after a child. The little girls that I meet in the little streets of Battersea worship their dolls in a way that reminds one not so much of play as idolatry. In some cases the love and care of the artistic symbol has actually become more important than the human reality which it was, I suppose, originally meant to symbolise.

I remember a Battersea little girl who wheeled her large baby sister stuffed into a doll's perambulator. When questioned on this course of conduct, she replied: 'I haven't got a dolly, and Baby is pretending to be my dolly.' Nature was indeed imitating art. First a doll had been a substitute for a child; afterwards a child was a mere substitute for a doll. But that opens other matters; the point is here that such devotion takes up most of the brain and most of the life; much as if it were really the thing which it is supposed to symbolise. The point is that the man writing on motherhood is merely an educationalist; the child playing with a doll is a mother.

Take the case of soldiers. A man writing an article on military strategy is simply a man writing an article; a horrid sight. But a boy making a campaign with tin soldiers is like a General making a campaign with live soldiers. He must to the limit of his juvenile powers think about the thing; whereas the war correspondent need not think at all. I remember a war correspondent who remarked after the capture of Methuen: 'This renewed activity on the part of Delarey is probably due to his being short of stores.' The same military critic had mentioned a few paragraphs before that Delarey was being hard pressed by a column which was pursuing him under the command of Methuen. Methuen chased Delarey; and Delarey's activity was due to his being short of stores. Otherwise he would have stood quite still while he was chased. I run after Jones with a hatchet, and if he turns round and tries to get rid of me the only possible explanation is that he has a very small balance at his bankers. I cannot believe that any boy playing at soldiers would be as idiotic as this. But then any one playing at anything has to be serious. Whereas, as I have only too good reason to know, if you are writing an article you can say anything that comes into your head.

Broadly, then, what keeps adults from joining in children's games is, generally speaking, not that they have no pleasure in them; it is simply that they have no leisure for them. It is that they cannot afford the expenditure of toil and time and consideration for so grand and grave a scheme. I have been myself attempting for some time past to complete a play in a small toy theatre, the sort of toy theatre that used to be called Penny Plain and Twopence Coloured; only that I drew and coloured the figures and scenes myself. Hence I was free from the degrading obligation of having to pay either a penny or twopence; I only had to pay a shilling a sheet for good cardboard and a shilling a box for bad water colours. The kind of miniature stage I mean is probably familiar to every one; it is never more than a development of the stage which Skelt made and Stevenson celebrated.

But though I have worked much harder at the toy theatre than I ever worked at any tale or article, I cannot finish it; the work seems too heavy for me. I have to break off and betake myself to lighter employments; such as the biographies of great men. The play of 'St George and the Dragon', over which I have burnt the midnight oil (you must colour the thing by lamplight because that is how it will be seen), still lacks most conspicuously, alas! two wings of the Sultan's Palace, and also some comprehensible and workable way of getting up the curtain.

All this gives me a feeling touching the real meaning of immortality. In this world we cannot have pure pleasure. This is partly because pure pleasure would be dangerous to us and to our neighbours. But it is partly because pure pleasure is a great deal too much trouble. If I am ever in any other and better world, I hope that I shall have enough time to play with nothing but toy theatres; and I hope that I shall have enough divine and superhuman energy to act at least one play in them without a hitch.

Meanwhile the philosophy of toy theatres is worth anyone's consideration. All the essential morals which modern men

need to learn could be deduced from this toy. Artistically considered, it reminds us of the main principle of art, the principle
which is in most danger of being forgotten in our time. I mean
the fact that art consists of limitation; the fact that art is limitation. Art does not consist in expanding things. Art consists
of cutting things down, as I cut down with a pair of scissors
my very ugly figures of St George and the Dragon. Plato,
who liked definite ideas, would like my cardboard dragon; for
though the creature has few other artistic merits he is at least
dragonish. The modern philosopher, who likes infinity, is quite
welcome to a sheet of the plain cardboard. The most artistic
thing about the theatrical art is the fact that the spectator looks
at the whole thing through a window. This is true even of
theatres inferior to my own; even at the Court Theatre or
His Majesty's you are looking through a window; an unusually
large window. But the advantage of the small theatre exactly is
that you are looking through a small window. Has not every
one noticed how sweet and startling any landscape looks when
seen through an arch? This strong, square shape, this shutting
off of everything else is not only an assistance to beauty; it is
the essential of beauty. The most beautiful part of every picture
is the frame.

This especially is true of the toy theatre; that, by redu-
cing the scale of events it can introduce much larger events.
Because it is small it could easily represent the earthquake
in Jamaica. Because it is small it could easily represent the Day
of Judgment. Exactly in so far as it is limited, so far it could
play easily with falling cities or with falling stars. Meanwhile
the big theatres are obliged to be economical because they are
big. When we have understood this fact we shall have understood something of the reason why the world has always been
first inspired by small nationalities. The vast Greek philosophy
could fit easier into the small city of Athens than into the
immense Empire of Persia. In the narrow streets of Florence
Dante felt that there was room for Purgatory and Heaven and

Hell. He would have been stifled by the British Empire. Great empires are necessarily prosaic; for it is beyond human power to act a great poem upon so great a scale. You can only represent very big ideas in very small spaces. My toy theatre is as philosophical as the drama of Athens.

Some Policemen and a Moral

The other day I was nearly arrested by two excited policemen in a wood in Yorkshire. I was on a holiday, and was engaged in that rich and intricate mass of pleasures, duties, and discoveries which for the keeping off of the profane, we disguise by the exoteric name of Nothing. At the moment in question I was throwing a big Swedish knife at a tree, practising (alas, without success) that useful trick of knife-throwing by which men murder each other in Stevenson's romances.

Suddenly the forest was full of two policemen; there was something about their appearance in and relation to the greenwood that reminded me, I know not how, of some happy Elizabethan comedy. They asked what the knife was, who I was, why I was throwing it, what my address was, trade, religion, opinions on the Japanese war, name of favourite cat, and so on. They also said I was damaging the tree; which was, I am sorry to say, not true, because I could not hit it. The peculiar philosophical importance, however, of the incident was this. After some half hour's animated conversation, the exhibition of an envelope, an unfinished poem, which was read with great care, and, I trust, with some profit, and one or two other subtle detective strokes, the elder of the two knights became convinced that I really was what I professed to be, that I was a journalist, that I was on the *Daily News* (this was the real stroke; they were shaken with a terror common to all tyrants), that I lived in a particular place as stated, and that I was stopping with particular people in Yorkshire, who happened to be wealthy and well-known in the neighbourhood.

In fact the leading constable became so genial and complimentary at last that he ended up by representing himself as a reader of my work. And when that was said, everything was settled. They acquitted me and let me pass.

'But,' I said, 'what of this mangled tree? It was to the rescue of that Dryad, tethered to the earth, that you rushed like knights errant. You, the higher humanitarians, are not deceived by the seeming stillness of the green things, a stillness like the stillness of the cataract, a headlong and crashing silence. You know that a tree is but a creature tied to the ground by one leg. You will not let assassins with their Swedish daggers shed the green blood of such a being. But if so, why am I not in custody; where are my gyves? Produce, from some portion of your persons, my mouldy straw and my grated window. The facts of which I have just convinced you, that my name is Chesterton, that I am a journalist, that I am living with the well-known and philanthropic Mr Blank of Ilkley, cannot have anything to do with the question of whether I have been guilty of cruelty to vegetables. The tree is none the less damaged even though it may reflect with a dark pride that it was wounded by a gentleman connected with the Liberal press. Wounds in the bark do not more rapidly close up because they are inflicted by people who are stopping with Mr Blank of Ilkley. That tree, the ruin of its former self, the wreck of what was once a giant of the forest, now splintered and laid low by the brute superiority of a Swedish knife, that tragedy, constable, cannot be wiped out even by stopping for several months more with some wealthy person. It is incredible that you have no legal claim to arrest even the most august and fashionable persons on this charge. For if so, why did you interfere with me at all?'

I made the later and larger part of this speech to the silent wood, for the two policemen had vanished almost as quickly as they came. It is very possible, of course, that they were fairies. In that case the somewhat illogical character of their view of crime, law, and personal responsibility would find a bright and elfish explanation; perhaps if I had lingered in the glade till moonrise I might have seen rings of tiny policemen dancing on the sward; or running about with glow-worm belts, arresting grasshoppers for damaging blades of grass. But taking the bolder hypothesis, that they really were policemen, I find myself in a certain difficulty. I was certainly accused of something which was either an offence or was not. I was let off because I proved I was a guest at a big house. The inference seems painfully clear; either it is not a proof of infamy to throw a knife about in a lonely wood, or else it is a proof of innocence to know a rich man. Suppose a very poor person, poorer even than a journalist, a navvy or unskilled labourer, tramping in search of work, often changing his lodgings, often, perhaps, failing in his rent. Suppose he had been intoxicated with the green gaiety of the ancient wood. Suppose he had thrown knives at trees and could give no description of a dwelling place except that he had been fired out of the last. As I walked home through a cloudy and purple twilight I wondered how he would have got on.

Moral. We English are always boasting that we are very illogical; there is no great harm in that. There is no subtle spiritual evil in the fact that people always brag about their vices; it is when they begin to brag about their virtues that they become insufferable. But there is this to be said, that illogicality in your constitution or your legal methods may become very dangerous if there happens to be some great national vice or national temptation which many take advantage of the chaos. Similarly, a drunkard ought to have strict rules and hours; a temperate man may obey his instincts.

Take some absurd anomaly in the British law – the fact, for instance, that a man ceasing to be an MP has to become Steward of the Chiltern Hundreds, an office which I believe was intended originally to keep down some wild robbers near Chiltern, wherever that is. Obviously this kind of illogicality does not matter very much, for the simple reason that there is no great temptation to take advantage of it. Men retiring from Parliament do not have any furious impulse to hunt robbers in the hills. But if there were a real danger that wise, white-haired, venerable politicians taking leave of public life would desire to do this (if, for instance, there were any money in it), then clearly, if we went on saying that the illogicality did not matter, when (as a matter of fact) Sir Michael Hicks-Beach was hanging

Chiltern shopkeepers every day and taking their property, we should be very silly. The illogicality would matter, for it would have become an excuse for indulgence. It is only the very good who can live riotous lives.

Now this is exactly what is present in cases of police investigation such as the one narrated above. There enters into such things a great national sin, a far greater sin than drink – the habit of respecting a gentleman. Snobbishness has, like drink, a kind of grand poetry. And snobbishness has this peculiar and devilish quality of evil, that it is rampant among very kindly people, with open hearts and houses. But it is our great English vice; to be watched more fiercely than smallpox. If a man wished to hear the worst and wickedest thing in England summed up in casual English words, he would not find it in any foul oaths or ribald quarrelling. He would find it in the fact that the best kind of working man, when he wishes to praise any one, calls him 'a gentleman'. It never occurs to him that he might as well call him 'a marquis', or 'a privy councillor' – that he is simply naming a rank or class, not a phrase for a good man. And this perennial temptation to a shameful admiration, must, and, I think, does, constantly come in and distort and poison our police methods.

In this case we must be logical and exact; for we have to keep watch upon ourselves. The power of wealth, and that power at its vilest, is increasing in the modern world. A very good and just people, without this temptation, might not need, perhaps, to make clear rules and systems to guard themselves against the power of our great financiers. But that is because a very just people would have shot them long ago, from mere native good feeling.

The Little Birds Who Won't Sing

On my last morning on the Flemish coast, when I knew that
in a few hours I should be in England, my eye fell upon one of
the details of Gothic carving of which Flanders is full. I do not
know whether the thing is old, though it was certainly knocked
about and indecipherable, but at least it was certainly in the
style and tradition of the early Middle Ages. It seemed to represent men bending themselves (not to say twisting themselves) to certain primary employments. Some seemed to be
sailors tugging at ropes; others, I think, were reaping; others
were energetically pouring something into something else.
This is entirely characteristic of the pictures and carvings of the
early thirteenth century, perhaps the most purely vigorous time
in all history. The great Greeks preferred to carve their gods
and heroes doing nothing. Splendid and philosophic as their
composure is there is always about it something that marks
the master of many slaves. But if there was one thing the early
mediaevals liked it was representing people doing something –
hunting or hawking, or rowing boats, or treading grapes, or
making shoes, or cooking something in a pot. *'Quicquid agunt
homines, votum, timor, ira voluptas.'* (I quote from memory.)
The Middle Ages is full of that spirit in all its monuments
and manuscripts. Chaucer retains it in his jolly insistence on
everybody's type of trade and toil. It was the earliest and
youngest resurrection of Europe, the time when social order
was strengthening, but had not yet become oppressive; the time
when religious faiths were strong, but had not yet been exasper-
ated. For this reason the whole effect of Greek and Gothic
carving is different. The figures in the Elgin marbles, though
often reining their steeds for an instant in the air, seem frozen
for ever at that perfect instant. But a mass of medieval carving
seems actually a sort of bustle or hubbub in stone. Sometimes
one cannot help feeling that the groups actually move and

mix, and the whole front of a great cathedral has the hum of a huge hive.

But about these particular figures there was a peculiarity of which I could not be sure. Those of them that had any heads had very curious heads, and it seemed to me that they had their mouths open. Whether or no this really meant anything or was an accident of nascent art I do not know; but in the course of wondering I recalled to my mind the fact that singing was connected with many of the tasks there suggested, that there were songs for reapers and songs for sailors hauling ropes. I was still thinking about this small problem when I walked along the pier at Ostend; and I heard some sailors uttering a measured shout as they laboured, and I remembered that sailors still sing in chorus while they work, and even sing different songs according to what part of their work they are doing. And a little while afterwards, when my sea journey was over, the sight of men working in the English fields reminded me again that there are still songs for harvest and for many agricultural routines. And I suddenly wondered why if this were so it should be quite unknown, for any modern trade to have a ritual poetry. How did people come to chant rude poems while pulling certain ropes or gathering certain fruit, and why did nobody do anything of the kind while producing any of the modern things? Why is a modern newspaper never printed by people singing in chorus? Why do shopmen seldom, if ever, sing?

If reapers sing while reaping, why should not auditors sing while auditing and bankers while banking? If there are songs for all the separate things that have to be done in a boat, why are there not songs for all the separate things that have to be done in a bank? As the train from Dover flew through the Kentish gardens, I tried to write a few songs suitable for commercial gentlemen. Thus, the work of bank clerks when casting up columns might begin with a thundering chorus in praise of Simple Addition.

Up my lads and lift the ledgers, sleep and ease are o'er.
  Hear the Stars of Morning shouting: 'Two and Two are
    four.'
Though the creeds and realms are reeling, though the sophists roar,
  Though we weep and pawn our watches, Two and Two are
    Four.

There's a run upon the Bank –
  Stand away!
For the Manager's a crank and the Secretary drank, and the
  Upper Tooting Bank
    Turns to bay!
Stand close: there is a run
  On the Bank.
Of our ship, our royal one, let the ringing legend run, that she
  fired with every gun
    Ere she sank.

And as I came into the cloud of London I met a friend of mine who actually is in a bank, and submitted these suggestions in rhyme to him for use among his colleagues. But he was not very hopeful about the matter. It was not (he assured me) that he underrated the verses, or in any sense lamented their lack of polish. No; it was rather, he felt, an indefinable something in the very atmosphere of the society in which we live that makes it spiritually difficult to sing in banks. And I think he must be right; though the matter is very mysterious. I may observe here that I think there must be some mistake in the calculations of the Socialists. They put down all our distress, not to a moral tone, but to the chaos of private enterprise. Now, banks are private; but post offices are socialistic: therefore I naturally expected that the post office would fall into the collectivist idea of a chorus. Judge of my surprise when the lady in my local post office (whom I urged to sing) dismissed the idea with far more coldness than the bank clerk had done. She seemed indeed, to be in a considerably greater state of depression than he. Should anyone suppose that this was the effect of the verses themselves, it is only fair to say that the specimen verse of the Post Office Hymn ran thus:

O'er London our letters are shaken like snow,
Our wires o'er the world like the thunderbolts go.
The news that may marry a maiden in Sark,
Or kill an old lady in Finsbury Park.

Chorus (with a swing of joy and energy):

Or kill an old lady in Finsbury Park.

And the more I thought about the matter the more painfully certain it seemed that the most important and typical modern things could not be done with a chorus. One could not, for instance, be a great financier and sing; because the essence of being a great financier is that you keep quiet. You could not even in many modern circles be a public man and sing; because in those circles the essence of being a public man is that you do nearly everything in private. Nobody would imagine a chorus of money lenders. Every one knows the story of the solicitors' corps of volunteers who, when the Colonel on the battlefield cried 'Charge!' all said simultaneously, 'Six-and-eightpence'. Men can sing while charging in a military, but hardly in a legal sense. And at the end of my reflections I had really got no further than the subconscious feeling of my friend the bank clerk – that there is something spiritually suffocating about our life; not about our laws merely, but about our life. Bank clerks are without songs, not because they are poor, but because they are sad. Sailors are much poorer. As I passed homewards I passed a little tin building of some religious sort, which was shaken with shouting as a trumpet is torn with its own tongue. *They* were singing anyhow; and I had for an instant a fancy I had often had before: that with us the superhuman is the only place where you can find the human. Human nature is hunted and has fled into sanctuary.

A Somewhat Improbable Story

I cannot remember whether this tale is true or not. If I read it through very carefully I have a suspicion that I should come to the conclusion that it is not. But, unfortunately, I cannot read it through very carefully, because, you see, it is not written yet. The image and the idea of it clung to me through a great part of my boyhood; I may have dreamt it before I could talk; or told it to myself before I could read; or read it before I could remember. On the whole, however, I am certain that I did not read it, for children have very clear memories about things like that; and of the books which I was really fond I can still remember, not only the shape and bulk and binding, but even the position of the printed words on many of the pages. On the whole, I incline to the opinion that it happened to me before I was born.

At any rate, let us tell the story now with all the advantages of the atmosphere that has clung to it. You may suppose me, for the sake of argument, sitting at lunch in one of those quick-lunch restaurants in the City where men take their food so fast that it has none of the quality of food, and take their half hour's vacation so fast that it has none of the qualities of leisure; to hurry through one's leisure is the most unbusinesslike of actions. They all wore tall shiny hats as if they could not lose an instant even to hang them on a peg, and they all had one eye a little off, hypnotised by the huge eye of the clock. In short, they were the slaves of the modern bondage, you could hear their fetters clanking. Each was, in fact, bound by a chain; the heaviest chain ever tied to a man – it is called a watch chain.

Now, among these there entered and sat down opposite to me a man who almost immediately opened an uninterrupted monologue. He was like all the other men in dress, yet he was startlingly opposite to them in all manner. He wore a high shiny hat and a long frock coat, but he wore them as such solemn things were meant to be worn; he wore the silk hat as if it were a mitre, and the frock coat as if it were the ephod of a high priest. He not only hung his hat up on the peg, but he seemed (such was his stateliness) almost to ask permission of the hat for doing so, and to apologise to the peg for making use of it. When he had sat down on a wooden chair with the air of one considering its feelings and given a sort of slight stoop or bow to the wooden table itself, as if it were an altar, I could not help some comment springing to my lips. For the man was a big, sanguine-faced, prosperous-looking man, and yet he treated everything with a care that almost amounted to nervousness.

For the sake of saying something to express my interest I said, 'This furniture is fairly solid; but, of course, people do treat it much too carelessly.'

As I looked up doubtfully my eye caught his, and was fixed as his was fixed in an apocalyptic stare. I had thought him ordinary as he entered, save for his strange, cautious manner; but if the other people had seen him then they would have screamed and emptied the room. They did not see him, and they went on making a clatter with their forks, and a murmur with their conversation. But the man's face was the face of a maniac.

'Did you mean anything particular by that remark?' he asked at last, and the blood crawled back slowly into his face.

'Nothing whatever,' I answered. 'One does not mean anything here; it spoils people's digestions.'

He limped back and wiped his broad forehead with a big handkerchief; and yet there seemed to be a sort of regret in his relief.

'I thought perhaps,' he said in a low voice, 'that another of them had gone wrong.'

'If you mean another digestion gone wrong,' I said, 'I never heard of one here that went right. This is the heart of the Empire, and the other organs are in an equally bad way.'

'No, I mean another street gone wrong,' and he said heavily and quietly, 'but as I suppose that doesn't explain much to you, I think I shall have to tell you the story. I do so with all the less responsibility, because I know you won't believe it. For forty years of my life I invariably left my office, which is in Leadenhall Street, at half past five in the afternoon, taking with me an umbrella in the right hand and a bag in the left hand. For forty years two months and four days I passed out of the side office door, walked down the street on the left-hand side, took the first turning to the left and the third to the right, from where I bought an evening paper, followed the road on the right-hand side round two obtuse angles, and came out just outside a Metropolitan station, where I took a train home. For forty years two months and four days I fulfilled this course by accumulated habit: it was not a long street that I traversed, and it took me about four and a half minutes to do it. After forty years two months and four days, on the fifth day I went out in the same manner, with my umbrella in the right hand and my bag in the left, and I began to notice that walking along the familiar street tired me somewhat more than usual; and when I turned it I was convinced that I had turned down the wrong one. For now the street shot up quite a steep slant, such as one only sees in the hilly parts of London, and in this part there were no hills at all. Yet it was not the wrong street; the name written on it was the same; the shuttered shops were the same; the lampposts and the whole look of the perspective was the same; only it was tilted upwards like a lid. Forgetting any trouble about breathlessness or fatigue I ran furiously forward, and reached the second of my accustomed turnings, which ought to bring me almost within sight of the station. And as I turned that corner I nearly fell on the pavement. For now the street went up straight in front of my face like a steep staircase or the side of a pyramid. There was not for miles round that place so much as a slope like that of Ludgate Hill. And this was a slope like that of the Matterhorn. The whole street had lifted itself like a single wave, and yet every speck and detail of it was the same, and I saw in the high distance, as at the top of an Alpine pass, picked out in pink letters the name over my paper shop.

'I ran on and on blindly now, passing all the shops and coming to a part of the road where there was a long grey row of private houses. I had, I know not why, an irrational feeling that I was a long iron bridge in empty space. An impulse seized me, and I pulled up the iron trap of a coal hole. Looking down through it I saw empty space and the stars.

'When I looked up again a man was standing in his front garden, having apparently come out of his house; he was leaning over the railings and gazing at me. We were all alone on that nightmare road; his face was in shadow; his dress was dark and ordinary; but when I saw him standing so perfectly still I knew somehow that he was not of this world. And the stars behind his head were larger and fiercer than ought to be endured by the eyes of men.

'"If you are a kind angel," I said, "or a wise devil, or have anything in common with mankind, tell me what is this street possessed of devils."

'After a long silence he said, "What do you say that it is?"

'"It is Bumpton Street, of course," I snapped. "It goes to Oldgate Station."

'"Yes," he admitted gravely, "it goes there sometimes. Just now, however, it is going to heaven."

'"To heaven?" I said. "Why?"

'"It is going to heaven for justice," he replied. "You must have treated it badly. Remember always that there is one thing that cannot be endured by anybody or anything. That one un-endurable thing is to be overworked and also neglected. For instance, you can overwork women – everybody does. But you can't neglect women – I defy you to. At the same time, you can neglect tramps and gypsies and all the apparent refuse of the State so long as you do not overwork it. But no beast of the field, no horse, no dog can endure long to be asked to do more than his work and yet have less than his honour. It is the same with streets. You have worked this street to death, and yet you have never remembered its existence. If you had a healthy democracy,

82

even of pagans, they would have hung this street with garlands and given it the name of a god. Then it would have gone quietly. But at last the street has grown tired of your tireless insolence; and it is bucking and rearing its head to heaven. Have you never sat on a bucking horse?"

'I looked at the long grey street, and for a moment it seemed to me to be exactly like the long grey neck of a horse flung up to heaven. But in a moment my sanity returned, and I said, "But this is all nonsense. Streets go to the place they have to go. A street must always go to its end."

'"Why do you think so of a street?" he asked, standing very still.

'"Because I have always seen it do the same thing," I replied, in reasonable anger. "Day after day, year after year, it has always gone to Oldgate Station; day after…"

'I stopped, for he had flung up his head with the fury of the road in revolt.

'"And you?" he cried terribly. "What do you think the road thinks of you? Does the road think you are alive? Are you alive? Day after day, year after year, you have gone to Oldgate Station…" Since then I have respected the things called inanimate.'

And bowing slightly to the mustard pot, the man in the restaurant withdrew.

The Shop Of Ghosts

Nearly all the best and most precious things in the universe you can get for a halfpenny. I make an exception, of course, of the sun, the moon, the earth, people, stars, thunderstorms, and such trifles. You can get them for nothing. Also I make an exception of another thing, which I am not allowed to mention in this paper, and of which the lowest price is a penny halfpenny. But the general principle will be at once apparent. In the street behind me, for instance, you can now get a ride on an electric tram for a halfpenny. To be on an electric tram is to be on a flying castle in a fairy tale. You can get quite a large number of brightly coloured sweets for a halfpenny. Also you can get the chance of reading this article for a halfpenny; along, of course, with other and irrelevant matter.

But if you want to see what a vast and bewildering array of valuable things you can get at a halfpenny each you should do as I was doing last night. I was gluing my nose against the glass of a very small and dimly lit toy shop in one of the greyest and leanest of the streets of Battersea. But dim as was that square of light, it was filled (as a child once said to me) with all the colours God ever made. Those toys of the poor were like the children who buy them; they were all dirty; but they were all bright. For my part, I think brightness more important than cleanliness; since the first is of the soul, and the second of the body. You must excuse me; I am a democrat; I know I am out of fashion in the modern world.

As I looked at that palace of pigmy wonders, at small green omnibuses, at small blue elephants, at small black dolls, and small red Noah's arks, I must have fallen into some sort of un-natural trance. That lit shop window became like the brilliantly lit stage when one is watching some highly coloured comedy. I forgot the grey houses and the grimy people behind me as one forgets the dark galleries and the dim crowds at a theatre.

It seemed as if the little objects behind the glass were small, not because they were toys, but because they were objects far away. The green omnibus was really a green omnibus, a green Bayswater omnibus, passing across some huge desert on its ordinary way to Bayswater. The blue elephant was no longer blue with paint; he was blue with distance. The black doll was really a negro relieved against passionate tropic foliage in the land where every weed is flaming and only man is black. The red Noah's ark was really the enormous ship of earthly salvation riding on the rain-swollen sea, red in the first morning of hope.

Every one, I suppose, knows such stunning instants of abstraction, such brilliant blanks in the mind. In such moments one can see the face of one's own best friend as an unmeaning pattern of spectacles or moustaches. They are commonly marked by the two signs of the slowness of their growth and the suddenness of their termination. The return to real thinking is often as abrupt as bumping into a man. Very often indeed (in my case) it is bumping into a man. But in any case the awakening is always emphatic and, generally speaking, it is always complete. Now, in this case, I did come back with a shock of sanity to the consciousness that I was, after all, only staring into a dingy little toy shop; but in some strange way the mental cure did not seem to be final. There was still in my mind an unmanageable something that told me that I had strayed into some odd atmosphere, or that I had already done some odd thing. I felt as if I had worked a miracle or committed a sin. It was as if I had at any rate, stepped across some border in the soul.

To shake off this dangerous and dreamy sense I went into the shop and tried to buy wooden soldiers. The man in the shop was very old and broken, with confused white hair covering his head and half his face, hair so startlingly white that it looked almost artificial. Yet though he was senile and even sick, there was nothing of suffering in his eyes; he looked rather as if he were gradually falling asleep in a not unkindly decay. He gave me the wooden soldiers, but when I put down the money he did not at first seem to see it; then he blinked at it feebly, and then he pushed it feebly away.

'No, no,' he said vaguely. 'I never have. I never have. We are rather old-fashioned here.'

'Not taking money,' I replied, 'seems to me more like an uncommonly new fashion than an old one.'

'I never have,' said the old man, blinking and blowing his nose, 'I've always given presents. I'm too old to stop.'

'Good heavens!' I said. 'What can you mean? Why, you might be Father Christmas.'

'I am Father Christmas,' he said apologetically, and blew his nose again.

The lamps could not have been lighted yet in the street outside. At any rate, I could see nothing against the darkness but the shining shop window. There were no sounds of steps or voices in the street; I might have strayed into some new and sunless world. But something had cut the chords of common sense, and I could not feel even surprise except sleepily. Something made me say, 'You look ill, Father Christmas.'

'I am dying,' he said.

I did not speak, and it was he who spoke again.

'All the new people have left my shop. I cannot understand it. They seem to object to me on such curious and inconsistent sort of grounds, these scientific men, and these innovators. They say that I give people superstitions and make them too visionary; they say I give people sausages and make them too coarse. They say my heavenly parts are too heavenly; they say my earthly parts are too earthly; I don't know what they want, I'm sure. How can heavenly things be too heavenly, or earthly things too earthly? How can one be too good, or too jolly? I don't understand. But I understand one thing well enough. These modern people are living and I am dead.'

'You may be dead,' I replied. 'You ought to know. But as for what they are doing, do not call it living.'

A silence fell suddenly between us which I somehow expected to be unbroken. But it had not fallen for more than a few seconds when, in the utter stillness, I distinctly heard a very rapid step coming nearer and nearer along the street. The next moment a figure flung itself into the shop and stood framed in the doorway. He wore a large white hat tilted back as if in impatience; he had tight black old-fashioned pantaloons, a gaudy old-fashioned stock and waistcoat, and an old fantastic coat. He had large, wide-open, luminous eyes like those of an arresting actor; he had a pale, nervous face, and a fringe of beard. He took in the shop and the old man in a look that seemed literally a flash and uttered the exclamation of a man utterly staggered.

'Good lord!' he cried out; 'it can't be you! It isn't you! I came to ask where your grave was.'

'I'm not dead yet, Mr Dickens,' said the old gentleman, with a feeble smile, 'but I'm dying,' he hastened to add reassuringly.

'But, dash it all, you were dying in my time,' said Mr Charles Dickens with animation, 'and you don't look a day older.'

'I've felt like this for a long time,' said Father Christmas.

Mr Dickens turned his back and put his head out of the door into the darkness.

'Dick,' he roared at the top of his voice, 'he's still alive.'

Another shadow darkened the doorway, and a much larger and more full-blooded gentleman in an enormous periwig came in, fanning his flushed face with a military hat of the cut of Queen Anne. He carried his head well back like a soldier, and his hot face had even a look of arrogance, which was suddenly contradicted by his eyes, which were literally as humble as a dog's. His sword made a great clatter, as if the shop were too small for it.

'Indeed,' said Sir Richard Steele, ''tis a most prodigious matter, for the man was dying when I wrote about Sir Roger de Coverley and his Christmas Day.'

My senses were growing dimmer and the room darker. It seemed to be filled with newcomers.

'It hath ever been understood,' said a burly man, who carried his head humorously and obstinately a little on one side – I think he was Ben Jonson – 'It hath ever been understood, consule Jacobo, under our King James and her late Majesty, that such good and hearty customs were fallen sick, and like to pass from the world. This grey beard most surely was no lustier when I knew him than now.'

And I also thought I heard a green-clad man, like Robin Hood, say in some mixed Norman French, 'But I saw the man dying.'

'I have felt like this a long time,' said Father Christmas, in his feeble way again.

Mr Charles Dickens suddenly leant across to him.

'Since when?' he asked. 'Since you were born?'

'Yes,' said the old man, and sank shaking into a chair. 'I have been always dying.'

Mr Dickens took off his hat with a flourish like a man calling a mob to rise.

'I understand it now,' he cried, 'you will never die.'

The Ballad of a Strange Town

My friend and I, in fooling about Flanders, fell into a fixed affection for the town of Mechlin or Malines. Our rest there was so restful that we almost felt it as a home, and hardly strayed out of it.

We sat day after day in the marketplace, under little trees growing in wooden tubs, and looked up at the noble converging lines of the Cathedral tower, from which the three riders from Ghent, in the poem, heard the bell which told them they were not too late. But we took as much pleasure in the people, in the little boys with open, flat Flemish faces and fur collars round their necks, making them look like burgomasters; or the women, whose prim, oval faces, hair strained tightly off the temples, and mouths at once hard, meek, and humorous, exactly reproduced the late mediaeval faces in Memling and Van Eyck.

But one afternoon, as it happened, my friend rose from under his little tree, and pointing to a sort of toy train that was puffing smoke in one corner of the clear square, suggested that we should go by it. We got into the little train, which was meant really to take the peasants and their vegetables to and fro from their fields beyond the town, and the official came round to give us tickets. We asked him what place we should get to if we paid fivepence. The Belgians are not a romantic people, and he asked us (with a lamentable mixture of Flemish coarseness and French rationalism) where we wanted to go.

We explained that we wanted to go to fairyland, and the only question was whether we could get there for fivepence. At last, after a great deal of international misunderstanding (for he spoke French in the Flemish and we in the English manner), he told us that fivepence would take us to a place which I have never seen written down, but which when spoken sounded like the word 'Waterloo' pronounced by an intoxicated patriot; I think it was Waerlowe.

We clasped our hands and said it was the place we had been seeking from boyhood, and when we had got there we descended with promptitude.

For a moment I had a horrible fear that it really was the field of Waterloo; but I was comforted by remembering that it was in quite a different part of Belgium. It was a crossroads, with one cottage at the corner, a perspective of tall trees like Hobbema's 'Avenue', and beyond only the infinite flat chessboard of the little fields. It was the scene of peace and prosperity; but I must confess that my friend's first action was to ask the man when there would be another train back to Mechlin. The man stated that there would be a train back in exactly one hour. We walked up the avenue, and when we were nearly half an hour's walk away it began to rain.

We arrived back at the crossroads sodden and dripping, and, finding the train waiting, climbed into it with some relief. The officer on this train could speak nothing but Flemish, but he understood the name Mechlin, and indicated that when we came to Mechlin Station he would put us down, which, after the right interval of time, he did.

We got down, under a steady downpour, evidently on the edge of Mechlin, though the features could not easily be recognised through the grey screen of the rain. I do not generally agree with those who find rain depressing. A shower-bath is not depressing; it is rather startling. And if it is exciting when a man throws a pail of water over you, why should it not also be exciting when the gods throw many pails? But on this soaking afternoon, whether it was the dull skyline of the Netherlands or the fact that we were returning home without any adventure, I really did think things a trifle dreary. As soon as we could creep under the shelter of a street we turned into a little café, kept by one woman. She was incredibly old, and she spoke no French. There we drank black coffee and what was called 'cognac fine'. 'Cognac fine' were the only two French words used in the establishment, and they were not true. At least, the fineness (perhaps by its very ethereal delicacy) escaped me. After a little my friend, who was more restless than I, got up and went out, to see if the rain had stopped and if we could at once stroll back to our hotel by the station. I sat finishing my coffee in a colourless mood, and listening to the unremitting rain.

Suddenly the door burst open, and my friend appeared, transfigured and frantic.

'Get up!' he cried, waving his hands wildly. 'Get up! We're in the wrong town! We're not in Mechlin at all. Mechlin is ten miles, twenty miles off – God knows what! We're somewhere near Antwerp.'

'What!' I cried, leaping from my seat, and sending the furniture flying. 'Then all is well, after all! Poetry only hid her face for an instant behind a cloud. Positively for a moment I was feeling depressed because we were in the right town. But if we are in the wrong town – why, we have our adventure after all! If we are in the wrong town, we are in the right place.'

I rushed out into the rain, and my friend followed me somewhat more grimly. We discovered we were in a town called Lierre, which seemed to consist chiefly of bankrupt pastry cooks, who sold lemonade.

'This is the peak of our whole poetic progress!' I cried enthusiastically. 'We must do something, something sacramental and commemorative! We cannot sacrifice an ox, and it would be a bore to build a temple. Let us write a poem.'

With but slight encouragement, I took out an old envelope and one of those pencils that turn bright violet in water. There was plenty of water about, and the violet ran down the paper, symbolising the rich purple of that romantic hour. I began, choosing the form of an old French ballad; it is the easiest because it is the most restricted –

Can Man to Mount Olympus rise,
*   And fancy Primrose Hill the scene?*
Can a man walk in Paradise
*   And think he is in Turnham Green?*
And could I take you for Malines,
*   Not knowing the nobler thing you were?*
O Pearl of all the plain, and queen,
*   The lovely city of Lierre.*

Through memory's mist in glimmering guise
*   Shall shine your streets of sloppy sheen.*
And wet shall grow my dreaming eyes,
*   To think how wet my boots have been*
Now if I die or shoot a Dean –

Here I broke off to ask my friend whether he thought it expressed a more wild calamity to shoot a Dean or to be a Dean. But he only turned up his coat collar, and I felt that for him the muse had folded her wings. I rewrote –

Now if I die a Rural Dean,
*   Or rob a bank I do not care,*
Or turn a Tory. I have seen
*   The lovely city of Lierre.*

'The next line,' I resumed, warming to it; but my friend interrupted me.

'The next line,' he said somewhat harshly, 'will be a railway line. We can get back to Mechlin from here, I find, though we have to change twice. I dare say I should think this jolly romantic but for the weather. Adventure is the champagne of life, but I prefer my champagne and my adventures dry. Here is the station.'

We did not speak again until we had left Lierre, in its sacred cloud of rain, and were coming to Mechlin, under a clearer sky, that even made one think of stars. Then I leant forward and said to my friend in a low voice, 'I have found out everything. We have come to the wrong star.'

He stared his query, and I went on eagerly: 'That is what makes life at once so splendid and so strange. We are in the wrong world. When I thought that was the right town, it bored me; when I knew it was wrong, I was happy. So the false optimism, the modern happiness, tires us because it tells us we fit into this world. The true happiness is that we don't fit. We come from somewhere else. We have lost our way.'

He silently nodded, staring out of the window, but whether I had impressed or only fatigued him I could not tell. 'This,' I added, 'is suggested in the last verse of a fine poem you have grossly neglected –

"Happy is he and more than wise
  Who sees with wondering eyes and clean
The world through all the grey disguise
  Of sleep and custom in between.

Yes; we may pass the heavenly screen,
  But shall we know when we are there?
Who know not what these dead stones mean,
  The lovely city of Lierre."

Here the train stopped abruptly. And from Mechlin church steeple we heard the half chime: and Joris broke silence with 'No bally *hors d'oeuvres* for me: I shall get on to something solid at once.'

L'Envoy

Prince, wide your Empire spreads, I ween,
  Yet happier is that moistened Mayor,
Who drinks her cognac far from fine,
  The lovely city of Lierre.

Biographical note

Gilbert Keith Chesterton was born in 1874 in Campden Hill in Kensington, London and was educated at St Paul's School. He went on to attend illustration classes at the Slade School of Art and also to study literature at University College London.

Chesterton made his name as a journalist, a job he termed 'the easiest of all professions'. He worked at first as a freelance art and literary critic, and in 1902 was offered a weekly column in the *Daily News*. Later, in 1905, he began a column in *The Illustrated London News*, for which he would write for the next thirty years. He also wrote with Hilaire Belloc at *The Speaker*, a partnership that led Bernard Shaw to coin the term 'Chesterbelloc', and he contributed regularly to the *Eye Witness*, later renamed *New Witness*. In 1925 he founded his own newspaper, *G.K.'s Weekly*, which ran until 1936.

As well as a journalist, Chesterton was a prolific writer of novels, plays and literary criticism. His first novel, *The Napoleon of Notting Hill*, was published in 1904 and in 1912 came the first appearance of Chesterton's famous Father Brown in *The Innocence of Father Brown*. His poetry tended to celebrate Englishness, for example in 'The Rolling English Road' (1914), while his literary criticism included works on Robert Browning (1903) and Bernard Shaw (1910) and a much-admired book on Dickens (1906). He also published many volumes of religious, social and political essays, including *Orthodoxy* (1909) and *The Everlasting Man* (1925). His *Autobiography* appeared in 1936.

Chesterton converted to Catholicism in 1922 and died in 1936 at his home in Beaconsfield, Buckinghamshire, where he is buried in the Catholic cemetery.

HESPERUS PRESS

Hesperus Press, as suggested by the Latin motto, is committed to bringing near what is far – far both in space and time. Works written by the greatest authors, and unjustly neglected or simply little known in the English-speaking world, are made accessible through new translations and a completely fresh editorial approach. Through these classic works, the reader is introduced to the greatest writers from all times and all cultures.

For more information on Hesperus Press, please visit our website: **www.hesperuspress.com**

ET REMOTISSIMA PROPE

SELECTED TITLES FROM HESPERUS PRESS

'on'

Author	Title	Foreword writer
John Donne	*On Death*	Edward Docx
William Hazlitt	*On the Elgin Marbles*	Tom Paulin
John Stuart Mill	*On the Subjection of Women*	Fay Weldon
Virginia Woolf	*On Not Knowing Greek*	

Classics, Modern Voices and Brief Lives

Author	Title	Foreword writer
Jane Austen	*The Watsons*	Kate Atkinson
Edward Bulwer-Lytton	*The Coming Race*	Matthew Sweet
G.K. Chesterton	*The Club of Queer Trades*	Gilbert Adair
Arthur Conan Doyle	*The Tragedy of the Korosko*	Tony Robinson
Charles Dickens	*Mrs Lirriper*	Philip Hensher
Melissa Valiska Gregory and Melisa Klimaszewski	*Brief Lives: Charles Dickens*	
E.M. Forster	*Arctic Summer*	Anita Desai
Graham Greene	*No Man's Land*	David Lodge
Jerome K. Jerome	*The Idle Thoughts of an Idle Fellow*	
Charles Lamb	*Essays of Elia*	Matthew Sweet
Bernard Shaw	*The Adventures of the Black Girl in Her Search for God*	Colm Toíbín
Oscar Wilde	*The Portrait of Mr W.H.*	Peter Ackroyd
Richard Canning	*Brief Lives: Oscar Wilde*	
Virginia Woolf	*Hyde Park Gate News*	Hermione Lee